Best of PERUVIAN

Comforts made simple

GARDEN of GRAPES.

First Edition: 2023

Published by Garden of Grapes.

Printed in USA

The recipes, techniques, and tips in this cookbook are intended for personal use only. The author and publisher are not responsible for any adverse effects or consequences resulting from the use of the recipes or suggestions in this book.

Library of Congress Cataloging-in-Publication Data:

First edition.
Includes index.

Manufactured in USA

Introduction

Ladies and gentlemen, fellow lovers of good food and culinary explorers,

Welcome, with open arms and an eager appetite, to the "Peruvian Comforts Cookbook: Savor Peruvian Flavors." It's an absolute pleasure to have you join me on this flavorful journey into the heart of Peruvian cuisine, where tradition meets innovation, and where every dish tells a story of a vibrant and diverse culinary heritage.

Now, you might wonder, "Why Peru?" Well, the answer is as complex and captivating as the dishes you'll find within these pages. Peru, a country nestled along the Pacific coast of South America, is a place where geography, history, and culture have converged to create one of the world's most remarkable culinary landscapes. It's a land of ancient traditions blended with Spanish, African, Asian, and Indigenous influences, resulting in a tapestry of flavors that is nothing short of extraordinary.

My inspiration for crafting this cookbook comes from a deep love and admiration for Peruvian cuisine. I've had the privilege of wandering through bustling markets in Lima, where the air is thick with the scents of fresh seafood and exotic fruits. I've dined in humble picanterías, savoring dishes that have been perfected over generations. And I've marveled at the creativity of Peruvian chefs who are pushing the boundaries of what's possible in the kitchen.

In the "Peruvian Comforts Cookbook," you can expect to find a treasure trove of recipes that capture the essence of Peruvian gastronomy. From the iconic ceviche, where tender fish meets zesty lime and fiery chili, to the comforting embrace of a steaming bowl of aji de gallina, where tender chicken is swathed in a velvety, yellow pepper sauce—every dish is a celebration of Peru's culinary diversity.

Throughout these pages, I'll guide you through the preparation of these dishes with easy-to-follow instructions and beautiful, mouthwatering images to accompany each recipe. Whether you're a seasoned home cook or just beginning your culinary journey, you'll find something to delight your senses and satisfy your cravings.

So, my fellow food enthusiasts, as you turn the pages of this cookbook, I encourage you to embark on your own culinary adventure through Peru's rich and flavorful tapestry. Bring the vibrant tastes of Peru to your kitchen, share them with loved ones, and let these recipes transport you to the bustling streets of Lima, the lush Amazon rainforest, and the high Andes. May you savor every bite, appreciate every moment, and be inspired to create your own delicious memories.

With that, let the journey begin, and may your kitchen be filled with the vibrant and unforgettable flavors of Peru. ¡Buen provecho! (Enjoy your meal!)

Peruvian Chicken Soup

See page, 24

Cooking Philosophy or Approach

Ladies and gentlemen, fellow culinary explorers,

As we delve into the aromatic pages of the "Peruvian Comforts Cookbook: Savor Peruvian Flavors - 100+ Authentic Recipes," I'd like to share with you not just the delightful dishes of Peru but also the underlying philosophy that guided my approach to crafting this culinary journey.

Cooking, to me, has always been a remarkable fusion of art and science, tradition and innovation, and above all, an expression of culture and history. In the case of Peruvian cuisine, it's a tantalizing blend of ancient Inca traditions, Spanish influence, African heritage, and immigrant contributions, all woven together like the vibrant threads of a tapestry.

My approach to this cookbook was rooted in the deep respect and admiration I hold for Peruvian cuisine. It's a cuisine that has evolved over centuries, a testament to the diverse ecosystems and cultures that have thrived within the borders of this breathtaking country. Peru's cuisine is a tapestry of flavors, and in this cookbook, I aimed to capture not just the taste but also the essence of Peru.

One of the defining features of Peruvian cooking is its fearless use of bold flavors. From the fiery heat of ají amarillo peppers to the umami richness of Peruvian black mint (huacatay) to the citrusy zing of key limes, every ingredient is carefully selected to create a symphony of tastes that dance on the palate. The recipes in this cookbook are a celebration of these flavors, and I encourage you to embrace them with an open heart and an adventurous spirit.

Peruvian cuisine is also known for its reverence for tradition. In this cookbook, you'll find cherished recipes passed down through generations, dishes that have become an integral part of Peruvian culture. I've strived to maintain the authenticity of these recipes while making them accessible to home cooks around the world. Whether you're preparing a comforting plate of lomo saltado or diving into the irresistible world of ceviche, you'll find that the heart and soul of Peru are present in every bite.

But tradition doesn't mean stagnation. Peruvian cuisine is also a playground for culinary innovation. You'll discover a fusion of flavors and techniques that reflect the country's vibrant and ever-evolving food scene. From the tantalizing tiraditos that flirt with Japanese influences to the modern takes on classic causa, this cookbook invites you to explore the dynamic nature of Peruvian cooking.

In every recipe, I've aimed to strike a balance between preserving tradition and encouraging experimentation. I hope these dishes transport you to the bustling streets of Lima, the lush valleys of Cusco, and the coastal towns where the scent of the ocean mingles with the aroma of sizzling anticuchos. I hope you find in these pages the joy of discovery, the warmth of Peruvian hospitality, and the magic of a cuisine that has captivated the world.

So, as you embark on this culinary adventure through Peru, remember to savor not just the flavors but also the stories, the history, and the spirit of a nation expressed through its food. May your kitchen be filled with the vibrant and soulful flavors of Peru, and may each dish be a testament to the rich tapestry of Peruvian cuisine. ¡Buen provecho! (Enjoy your meal!)

Peruvian Estofado

See page, 33

Tips for Successful Cooking

Ladies and gentlemen, fellow culinary explorers,

Before we dive headfirst into the vibrant world of Peruvian cuisine within the pages of the "Peruvian Comforts Cookbook: Savor Peruvian Flavors - 100+ Authentic Recipes," I feel compelled to offer you some sage advice—wisdom that has been gleaned from my travels, my experiences in kitchens around the world, and my unwavering passion for the art of cooking.

Tip #1: Embrace the Peruvian Palette of Ingredients

Peruvian cuisine is a symphony of flavors, and at its heart are the diverse ingredients that this beautiful country has to offer. From the freshest seafood of the coastal regions to the robust potatoes of the Andes and the exotic fruits of the Amazon rainforest, Peruvian cooking is a celebration of biodiversity. So, when you embark on these culinary adventures, be sure to seek out the freshest and most authentic ingredients. Don't be afraid to explore local markets; they are treasure troves of Peruvian delights.

Tip #2: Master the Art of Ceviche

Ceviche, the iconic Peruvian dish, is a must-know for any aspiring Peruvian home chef. While the basic concept is simple—fresh seafood "cooked" in citrus juices—the variations are endless. The key is to use impeccably fresh seafood and to balance the acidity of the lime or lemon juice with the subtle heat of Peruvian chili peppers. Take your time, taste as you go, and you'll create a dish that dances on your taste buds.

Tip #3: Respect the Heat of Peruvian Peppers

Peruvian cuisine is known for its love affair with chili peppers, and rightly so. From the mild aji amarillo to the fiery rocoto, these peppers are the soul of Peruvian spice. When using them in your recipes, remember that the heat level can vary, so start with a little and adjust to your taste. Don't forget to remove the seeds and membranes if you want to tone down the heat.

Tip #4: Embrace the Pisco Sour

No journey through Peruvian cuisine would be complete without a taste of the famous Pisco Sour. This cocktail, a harmonious blend of Pisco (a grape brandy), lime juice, simple syrup, and egg white, is a testament to the artistry of Peruvian mixology. Learn to make it well, and you'll have the perfect accompaniment to your Peruvian feasts.

Tip #5: Learn the Art of Lomo Saltado

Lomo Saltado, a tantalizing stir-fry of beef, onions, tomatoes, and Peruvian spices, is a Peruvian comfort food classic. Master this dish, and you'll have a crowd-pleaser that captures the essence of Peruvian cuisine.

Tip #6: Embrace the Fusion of Flavors

Peruvian cuisine is a melting pot of influences, from the indigenous flavors of the Andes to the culinary traditions brought by immigrants from Europe, Asia, and Africa. Don't be afraid to experiment and create your own fusion of flavors. Peruvian cuisine is all about bold combinations.

As you embark on this culinary journey through Peru, remember that the heart of cooking lies not just in following recipes but in the joy of exploration and the sharing of good food with loved ones. So, savor each moment, each flavor, and each dish. Let the spirit of Peru infuse your cooking, and you'll create a symphony of flavors that will transport you straight to the heart of this beautiful country.

Buena suerte, and may your Peruvian cooking adventures be filled with delicious discoveries and unforgettable meals!

Peruvian Chupe de Gallina

See page, 30

Kitchen Essentials

My friends, before we dive into the vibrant world of Peruvian cuisine, let's talk about the tools that will be your trusty companions on this culinary journey. In any kitchen, be it a Michelin-starred restaurant or your cozy home, having the right equipment can make all the difference. So, here's a rundown of the kitchen essentials you'll want to have at your fingertips as you savor the flavors of Peru.

1. Chef's Knife: Think of it as your culinary sword. A sharp, high-quality chef's knife is your best friend in the kitchen. Use it for chopping, slicing, and dicing everything from onions to potatoes. Keep it honed for precision.

2. Cutting Board: To complement that trusty knife, you'll need a sturdy cutting board. Opt for one made of wood or plastic, depending on your preference, to protect both your knife and your countertop.

3. Blender or Food Processor: In Peruvian cooking, we often blend ingredients to create luscious sauces and marinades. A reliable blender or food processor is essential for achieving the right consistency in dishes like aji amarillo sauce or huacatay sauce.

4. Mortar and Pestle: If you want to go old-school and really connect with the heart of Peruvian cuisine, a mortar and pestle is a must. It's perfect for grinding spices and herbs to release their full flavor potential.

5. Potato Peeler: Potatoes are a cornerstone of Peruvian cuisine, and a good peeler will save you time and effort when preparing dishes like papas a la huancaina or causa limeña.

6. Rice Cooker: Perfectly cooked rice is crucial in Peruvian cooking. A rice cooker ensures consistently fluffy and flavorful grains for dishes like arroz con pollo.

7. Potato Ricer: For those lusciously creamy mashed potatoes or the essential base of a causa, a potato ricer is your secret weapon.

8. Large Pot and Skillet: A large, heavy-bottomed pot and a trusty skillet are indispensable for preparing Peruvian stews, searing meats, and more.

9. Grill or Grill Pan: If you're going for that authentic Peruvian grilled chicken or anticuchos, having a grill or grill pan is essential for achieving those smoky, charred flavors.

10. Citrus Juicer: Citrus fruits like limes and oranges are used liberally in Peruvian cuisine. A citrus juicer ensures you get every drop of that zesty goodness.

Now, let me share a few tips on how to make the most of these kitchen essentials. First and foremost, keep your knives sharp. A dull knife is not only frustrating but also potentially dangerous. Invest in a quality knife sharpener or take them to a professional.

When using your blender or food processor, start with the lowest speed and gradually increase to avoid splatters. For the mortar and pestle, use a gentle, grinding motion to release the flavors of herbs and spices.

Lastly, maintain your equipment. Regular cleaning and proper storage will extend the life of your kitchen tools, ensuring they're always ready for your next Peruvian culinary adventure.

With these kitchen essentials and a dash of passion, you're well-equipped to explore the diverse and delectable flavors of Peru. So, sharpen those knives, fire up the blender, and let's get cooking!

Flavor Pairing Suggestions

Ah, flavor pairing—what a glorious dance of tastes and textures that can turn a simple meal into a symphony of culinary delight. In the "Peruvian Comforts Cookbook: Savor Peruvian Flavors," we've journeyed through the vibrant and diverse world of Peruvian cuisine. Now, it's time to empower you, the adventurous home chef, to unleash your creativity and craft your own Peruvian-inspired masterpieces.

Peruvian cuisine is a tapestry of flavors, influenced by its indigenous roots, Spanish conquerors, African slaves, and immigrants from China and Japan. It's a cuisine that thrives on the harmony of contrasting tastes, and here, we'll explore some flavor pairing suggestions to inspire your culinary experiments.

1. Lime and Aji Amarillo: The zesty brightness of fresh lime juice pairs beautifully with the fruity heat of Aji Amarillo, the Peruvian yellow chili pepper. Use this combination as a marinade for grilled chicken or seafood, or drizzle it over ceviche for a burst of flavor.

2. Cilantro and Red Onion: Cilantro is the herbaceous heart of many Peruvian dishes, and its freshness complements the sharp bite of red onions. Try them together in a salsa criolla to top grilled meats, or use them as a garnish for your favorite Peruvian soups.

3. Corn and Queso Fresco: Corn is a Peruvian staple, and its natural sweetness pairs wonderfully with the mild, slightly salty queso fresco. Serve a warm corn salad with crumbled queso fresco for a delightful side dish.

4. Garlic and Paprika: A garlic and paprika paste, known as "adobo," is a cornerstone of Peruvian seasoning. It's versatile and adds depth to everything from roasted vegetables to meats. Experiment with the ratios to find your preferred level of smokiness and spice.

5. Chocolate and Chili: In Peruvian cuisine, chocolate isn't just for desserts. It's often used in savory dishes, where its bitterness complements the heat of chili peppers. Try adding a bit of dark chocolate to your chili or mole sauces for a rich, complex flavor.

6. Potatoes and Huancaina Sauce: Potatoes are a sacred ingredient in Peru, and huancaina sauce, made with cheese, yellow chili, and evaporated milk, is a luscious accompaniment. Top your boiled or roasted potatoes with this creamy sauce for a comforting side dish.

7. Lomo Saltado Fusion: This is a classic Peruvian stir-fry dish that combines beef, tomatoes, onions, and French fries. For a twist, experiment with adding soy sauce, ginger, and garlic for a fusion of Peruvian and Chinese flavors.

8. Plantains and Rocoto Sauce: Sweet and ripe plantains find their spicy match in rocoto sauce, made from rocoto chili peppers. Serve fried plantains with a drizzle of this fiery sauce for a tantalizing snack.

Remember, these are just starting points. Peruvian cuisine is all about exploration and the joy of discovering new combinations. So, don your apron, grab your ingredients, and embark on your own flavor adventure. The culinary canvas is yours to paint, and the flavors of Peru are your palette. Happy cooking!

Table of contents

Chapter 1:
Breakfast

2 tamales

350 cal

90 mins

Peruvian Tamales

Discover the heart of Peru with these steamed bundles of joy, filled with marinated pork and spices.

Ingredients:

- 4 cups masa harina
- 1 cup chicken broth
- 1 lb marinated pork
- 2 boiled eggs
- 4 olives
- 4 dried corn husks

Directions

1. Soak corn husks in warm water until pliable.
2. Mix masa harina and chicken broth to form dough.
3. Spread masa on corn husks.
4. Add pork, eggs, and olives.
5. Fold and steam for 60-75 mins.
6. Serve warm. Enjoy!

Substitutions

- Substitute pork with chicken.

1 serving

480 cal

60 mins

Easy

Chicharrón con Tamales

This indulgent combo features crispy fried pork, paired perfectly with tamales. A true Peruvian delight.

Ingredients:

- 2 slices fried pork belly
- 2 Peruvian tamales

Directions

1. Fry pork belly until crispy.
2. Heat tamales in steamer.
3. Serve tamales with pork slices.
4. Savor the deliciousness!

1 sandwic h

420 cal

20 mins

Easy

Pan con Chicharrón

Sink your teeth into this iconic Peruvian pork sandwich, bursting with flavors that'll make your day.

Ingredients:

- 1 Peruvian bread roll
- 2 slices fried pork belly
- Salsa criolla (Onion relish)

Directions

1. Slice bread roll in half.
2. Layer pork slices.
3. Top with salsa criolla.
4. Close and enjoy this heavenly sandwich!

Substitutions

- Use roast pork instead.

1 sandwic h

350 cal

15 mins

Butifarra

Originating from Lima, the Butifarra sandwich is a mouthwatering blend of ham and creamy Peruvian sauces.

Ingredients:

- 1 Peruvian bread roll
- 2 slices Peruvian ham
- Peruvian mayonnaise
- Peruvian mustard

Directions

1. Split the bread roll.
2. Spread mayo and mustard.
3. Layer with ham slices.
4. Savor the cultural flavors!

Substitutions

- Use regular ham and condiments.

6 sticks

280 cal

30 mins

Tequeños

These crispy cheese sticks are an irresistible snack, perfect for sharing and dipping in your favorite sauce.

Ingredients:

- 1 cup queso fresco (fresh cheese)
- 1 cup all-purpose flour
- 1 egg
- 1/2 cup milk
- Oil for frying

Directions

1. Mix cheese, flour, egg, and milk into dough.
2. Form sticks.
3. Fry until golden.
4. Serve with sauce and enjoy!

Substitutions

- Use mozzarella cheese.

1 serving

240 cal

15 mins

Peruvian Scrambled Eggs

Revuelto de Huevo is a simple yet comforting breakfast dish, featuring fluffy eggs with tomatoes and onions.

Ingredients:

- 2 eggs
- 1 tomato
- 1/4 onion
- Salt and pepper
- Oil for cooking

Directions

1. Sauté onions and tomatoes in oil.
2. Whisk eggs, salt, and pepper.
3. Pour over veggies, scramble.
4. Serve hot and enjoy!

Substitutions

- Add bell peppers for variation.

2 slices

320 cal

20 mins

Peruvian French Toast

Transform ordinary bread into a Peruvian delight with this cinnamon and vanilla-infused French toast recipe.

Ingredients:

- 4 slices Peruvian bread
- 2 eggs
- 1/2 cup milk
- 1 tsp vanilla extract
- 1 tsp ground cinnamon
- Butter for cooking

Directions

1. Whisk eggs, milk, vanilla, and cinnamon.
2. Dip bread slices.
3. Cook in butter until golden.
4. Serve hot with syrup. Enjoy!

Substitutions

- Use regular bread.

1 serving

220 cal

25 mins

Easy

Peruvian Quinoa Porridge

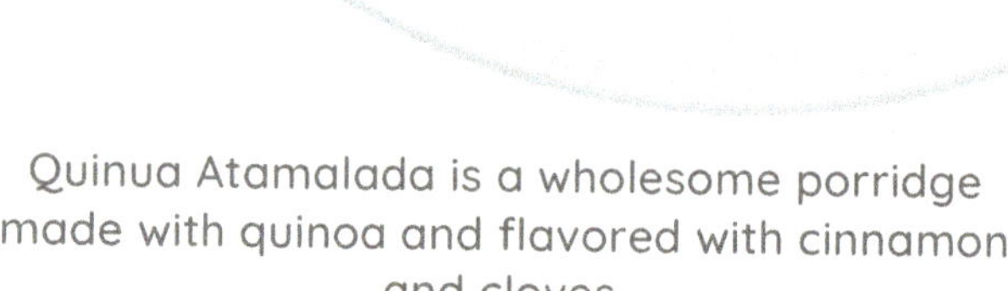

Quinua Atamalada is a wholesome porridge made with quinoa and flavored with cinnamon and cloves.

Ingredients:

- 1/2 cup quinoa
- 2 cups water
- 1/4 cup milk
- 1 cinnamon stick
- 3 cloves
- Sugar to taste

Directions

1. Rinse quinoa. Boil with water, cinnamon, and cloves.
2. Simmer until quinoa is tender.
3. Add milk and sugar.
4. Serve warm. Enjoy!

Substitutions

- Use almond milk for a twist.

2 cakes

280 cal

60 mins

Humitas Saladas

These savory corn cakes are a traditional Peruvian delicacy, made with corn masa and seasoned with aji amarillo.

Ingredients:

- 2 cups fresh corn masa
- 2 tbsp aji amarillo paste
- 1/4 cup grated cheese
- Salt
- Banana leaves

Directions

1. Mix corn masa, aji amarillo, cheese, and salt.
2. Spread on banana leaves.
3. Fold into packets.
4. Steam for 45 mins.
5. Enjoy!

Substitutions

- Use corn husks if leaves unavailable.

1 cup

200 cal

10 mins

Easy

Peruvian Hot Chocolate

Indulge in the warmth of Peruvian hot chocolate, a delightful blend of dark chocolate and spices.

Ingredients:

- 2 oz dark chocolate
- 2 cups milk
- 2 tsp sugar
- 1/2 tsp cinnamon
- 1/4 tsp vanilla extract

Directions

1. Melt chocolate in milk, sugar, cinnamon, and vanilla.
2. Whisk until smooth.
3. Pour into a cup and savor the richness. Enjoy!

Substitutions

- Add a pinch of chili powder.

Chapter 2:
Appetizers and Snacks

2 servings

360 cal

45 mins

Peruvian Causa Rellena

Causa Rellena is a stunning layered potato dish filled with chicken or tuna salad, showcasing the artistry of Peruvian cuisine.

Ingredients:

- 4 yellow potatoes
- 1/2 cup yellow chili pepper paste
- 2 limes
- 1 cup mayonnaise
- 1/2 cup cooked chicken or tuna
- 2 boiled eggs
- 1 avocado
- Lettuce leaves

Directions

1. Boil, peel, and mash potatoes. Mix with chili paste, lime juice, and salt.
2. Layer potato mixture, chicken/tuna salad, eggs, and avocado.
3. Chill and serve on lettuce leaves. Enjoy!

Substitutions

- Use aji amarillo if unavailable.

2 servings

380 cal

30 mins

Papa a la Huancaina (Potatoes)

Sliced boiled potatoes dressed in a creamy cheese sauce with a spicy kick, this dish from Huancayo is a flavor explosion on a plate.

Ingredients:

- 4 yellow potatoes
- 1 cup fresh cheese
- 4 yellow chili peppers
- 2 garlic cloves
- 1 cup evaporated milk
- 2 soda crackers
- Lettuce leaves

Directions

1. Boil, peel, and slice potatoes. Arrange on lettuce leaves.
2. Blend cheese, chili peppers, garlic, milk, and crackers.
3. Pour sauce over potatoes.
4. Garnish with olives and eggs. Enjoy the spicy delight!

Substitutions

- Adjust chili peppers for heat.

4 skewers

280 cal

40 mins

Normal

Anticuchos (Beef Heart Skewers)

Savor the bold flavors of Peru with these marinated beef heart skewers, a beloved street food tradition.

Ingredients:

- 1 lb beef heart
- 1/4 cup aji panca paste
- 2 garlic cloves
- 1/4 cup vinegar
- 2 tbsp vegetable oil
- Skewers

Directions

1. Cut beef heart into chunks.
2. Mix aji panca, garlic, vinegar, and oil to make marinade.
3. Marinate meat for 30 mins.
4. Thread onto skewers and grill until cooked.
5. Serve with boiled potatoes. Enjoy the Peruvian barbecue!

Substitutions

- Use beef sirloin if preferred.

6 empana das | 320 cal | 60 mins

Peruvian Empanadas

These flaky pastry pockets are filled with a delicious mixture of beef, olives, and raisins, offering a delightful blend of sweet and savory flavors.

Ingredients:

- 2 cups all-purpose flour
- 1/2 cup butter
- 1/4 cup water
- 1 lb ground beef
- 1/2 cup chopped onions
- 2 hard-boiled eggs
- 1/4 cup black olives
- 2 tbsp raisins
- Oil for frying

Directions

1. Mix flour and butter until crumbly. Add water to form dough.
2. Roll out dough and cut circles.
3. Cook beef and onions, then add eggs, olives, and raisins.
4. Fill dough circles, fold, and seal.
5. Fry until golden brown. Enjoy the sweet and savory goodness!

Substitutions

- Customize filling to taste.

6 sticks

280 cal

30 mins

Tequeños (Cheese Sticks)

These crispy cheese sticks are an irresistible snack, perfect for sharing and dipping in your favorite sauce.

Ingredients:

- 1 cup queso fresco (fresh cheese)
- 1 cup all-purpose flour
- 1 egg
- 1/2 cup milk
- Oil for frying

Directions

1. Mix cheese, flour, egg, and milk into dough.
2. Form sticks.
3. Fry until golden.
4. Serve with sauce and enjoy!

Substitutions

- Use mozzarella cheese.

2 servings | 320 cal | 20 mins

Easy

Peruvian Stuffed Avocado

Enjoy the creamy richness of ripe avocados stuffed with a zesty mixture of shrimp, onions, and mayo, a delightful appetizer or light meal.

Ingredients:

- 2 ripe avocados
- 1/2 lb cooked shrimp
- 1/4 cup chopped onions
- 1/4 cup mayonnaise
- 1 lime
- Salt and pepper

Directions

1. Cut avocados in half, remove pit, and scoop some flesh.
2. Mix shrimp, onions, mayo, lime juice, salt, and pepper.
3. Fill avocado halves.
4. Serve chilled and savor the creamy goodness!

Substitutions

- Substitute shrimp with crab.

4
potatoes

340 cal

60 mins

Normal

Papa Rellena (Stuffed Potatoes)

These crispy potato balls are stuffed with seasoned ground beef and hard-boiled eggs, making them a delightful Peruvian comfort food.

Ingredients:

- 4 large potatoes
- 1 lb ground beef
- 1/2 cup chopped onions
- 2 hard-boiled eggs
- 1/4 cup raisins
- 1/4 cup black olives
- Oil for frying

Directions

1. Boil, peel, and mash potatoes. Season with salt.
2. Cook beef and onions, then add eggs, raisins, and olives.
3. Form potato balls, stuff with filling.
4. Fry until golden brown. Enjoy the comforting delight!

Substitutions

- Customize filling to taste.

2 servings

260 cal

30 mins

Ceviche Mixto (Mixed Ceviche)

Dive into a refreshing dish of mixed seafood marinated in tangy lime juice, a classic Peruvian ceviche that's a burst of flavor in every bite.

Ingredients:

- 1/2 lb fish fillets
- 1/2 lb mixed seafood (shrimp, squid, octopus)
- 4 limes
- 1/2 red onion
- 1/2 aji limo (Peruvian chili)
- 1 sweet potato
- Lettuce leaves

Directions

1. Dice fish and seafood, marinate in lime juice.
2. Add diced onion and aji limo for heat.
3. Serve on lettuce leaves with boiled sweet potato.
4. Enjoy the zesty and refreshing flavors!

Substitutions

- Adjust chili for spiciness.

2 servings | 260 cal | 40 mins

Peruvian Yuquitas (Yuca Fries)

Yuquitas are crispy fried yuca fries, seasoned to perfection and served with a creamy dipping sauce, a favorite snack in Peru.

Ingredients:

- 1 lb yuca (cassava)
- Oil for frying
- Salt and pepper
- Huancaina sauce (optional, for dipping)

Directions

1. Peel yuca, cut into fries, and fry until golden.
2. Season with salt and pepper.
3. Serve with Huancaina sauce or your favorite dip.
4. Enjoy the crispy, flavorful yuca fries!

Substitutions

- Use yam or sweet potato.

1 serving

150 cal

15 mins

Peruvian Canchita (Toasted Corn)

Canchita is toasted corn, a crunchy and addictive Peruvian snack often enjoyed during movies or as a street food delight.

Ingredients:

- 1 cup giant corn kernels (mote)
- Oil for frying
- Salt

Directions

1. Heat oil in a pan, add corn kernels.
2. Fry until golden and crispy.
3. Drain excess oil, season with salt.
4. Enjoy the addictive crunch of Peruvian canchita!

Chapter 3:
Soups and Stews

4 servings

320 cal

45 mins

Normal

Peruvian Chicken Soup (Aguadito)

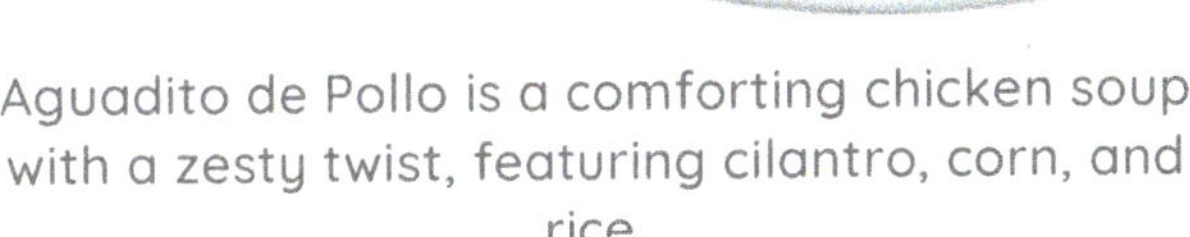
Aguadito de Pollo is a comforting chicken soup with a zesty twist, featuring cilantro, corn, and rice.

Ingredients:

- 1 lb chicken pieces
- 1 cup rice
- 1/2 cup green peas
- 1/2 cup corn kernels
- 1/4 cup cilantro
- 1/4 cup onion
- 2 garlic cloves
- 1 lime
- 8 cups chicken broth
- Salt and pepper

Directions

1. Sauté onion and garlic in a pot.
2. Add chicken, rice, peas, and corn.
3. Pour in chicken broth.
4. Simmer until rice is cooked.
5. Stir in cilantro, lime juice, salt, and pepper.
6. Serve hot. Enjoy the zesty chicken goodness!

Substitutions

- Use quail instead of chicken.

4
servings

280 cal

40 mins

Normal

Peruvian Fish Soup (Chupe)

Chupe de Pescado is a hearty fish soup enriched with vegetables, eggs, and a touch of cheese.

Ingredients:

- 1 lb white fish fillets
- 1/2 cup rice
- 1/2 cup green peas
- 1/2 cup carrots
- 1/4 cup diced tomatoes
- 1/4 cup onion
- 2 garlic cloves
- 2 eggs
- 1/4 cup cheese
- 8 cups fish broth
- Salt and pepper

Directions

1. Sauté onion and garlic in a pot.
2. Add rice, fish, peas, carrots, and tomatoes.
3. Pour in fish broth.
4. Simmer until rice is cooked.
5. Beat eggs, add to the soup.
6. Stir in cheese, salt, and pepper.
7. Serve hot. Enjoy the heartwarming fish soup!

Substitutions

- Use shrimp or seafood mix.

4 servings

340 cal

60 mins

Peruvian Beef Soup (Sopa Criolla)

Sopa Criolla is a rich beef soup with noodles, milk, and a poached egg, offering comfort in a bowl.

Ingredients:

- 1/2 lb beef sirloin
- 1/2 cup angel hair noodles
- 1/2 cup diced carrots
- 1/2 cup diced potatoes
- 1/4 cup chopped onions
- 2 garlic cloves
- 2 eggs
- 4 cups beef broth
- 1 cup milk
- Salt and pepper

Directions

1. Sauté onion and garlic in a pot.
2. Add beef, carrots, and potatoes.
3. Pour in beef broth and milk.
4. Simmer until beef is tender.
5. Cook noodles separately.
6. Poach eggs in the soup.
7. Season with salt and pepper.
8. Serve hot. Enjoy the comforting beef goodness!

Substitutions

- Use chicken for variation.

4
servings

320 cal

40 mins

Peruvian Shrimp Soup (Chupe)

Chupe de Camarones is a delightful shrimp soup with rice, vegetables, and a hint of fresh cheese.

Ingredients:

- 1/2 lb shrimp
- 1/2 cup rice
- 1/2 cup green peas
- 1/2 cup diced carrots
- 1/4 cup diced tomatoes
- 1/4 cup onion
- 2 garlic cloves
- 1/4 cup fresh cheese
- 8 cups shrimp or fish broth
- Salt and pepper

Directions

1. Sauté onion and garlic in a pot.
2. Add rice, shrimp, peas, carrots, and tomatoes.
3. Pour in broth.
4. Simmer until rice is cooked.
5. Stir in fresh cheese, salt, and pepper.
6. Serve hot. Enjoy the shrimp-infused goodness!

Substitutions

- Use fish or seafood mix.

4 servings

300 cal

30 mins

Easy

Peruvian Quinoa Soup (Sopa)

Sopa de Quinua is a nourishing quinoa soup enriched with vegetables, showcasing Peru's superfood.

Ingredients:

- 1/2 cup quinoa
- 1/2 cup diced carrots
- 1/2 cup diced potatoes
- 1/4 cup chopped onions
- 2 garlic cloves
- 8 cups vegetable or chicken broth
- Salt and pepper

Directions

1. Sauté onion and garlic in a pot.
2. Add quinoa, carrots, and potatoes.
3. Pour in broth.
4. Simmer until quinoa is cooked.
5. Season with salt and pepper.
6. Serve hot. Enjoy the nutritious quinoa soup!

Substitutions

- Add spinach or kale for greens.

4 servings

260 cal

40 mins

Easy

Peruvian Pumpkin Soup (Sopa)

Sopa de Zapallo is a creamy pumpkin soup with a touch of cheese and evaporated milk, a delightful treat.

Ingredients:

- 1 lb pumpkin
- 1/2 cup diced potatoes
- 1/4 cup chopped onions
- 2 garlic cloves
- 1/2 cup fresh cheese
- 1/2 cup evaporated milk
- 8 cups vegetable or chicken broth
- Salt and pepper

Directions

1. Sauté onion and garlic in a pot.
2. Add pumpkin, potatoes, and broth.
3. Simmer until pumpkin is tender.
4. Blend until smooth.
5. Stir in fresh cheese, milk, salt, and pepper.
6. Serve hot. Enjoy the creamy pumpkin delight!

Substitutions

- Use butternut squash.

4 servings | 360 cal | 60 mins

Normal

Peruvian Chupe de Gallina (Stew)

Chupe de Gallina is a hearty chicken stew with potatoes, eggs, and cheese, a deliciously comforting dish.

Ingredients:

- 1 lb chicken pieces
- 1/2 cup diced potatoes
- 1/4 cup diced carrots
- 1/4 cup chopped onions
- 2 garlic cloves
- 2 eggs
- 1/4 cup fresh cheese
- 4 cups chicken broth
- Salt and pepper

Directions

1. Sauté onion and garlic in a pot.
2. Add chicken, potatoes, and carrots.
3. Pour in broth.
4. Simmer until chicken is cooked.
5. Poach eggs in the soup.
6. Stir in fresh cheese, salt, and pepper.
7. Serve hot. Enjoy the heartwarming chicken stew!

Substitutions

- Use turkey for variation.

4 servings

380 cal

75 mins

Peruvian Carapulcra

Carapulcra is a traditional Peruvian stew made with dried potatoes and pork, simmered to perfection.

Ingredients:

- 1/2 lb pork loin
- 1/2 cup dried potatoes
- 1/4 cup aji panca paste
- 1/4 cup peanuts
- 1/4 cup chopped onions
- 2 garlic cloves
- 8 cups water
- 2 cups white wine
- Salt and pepper

Directions

1. Sauté onion and garlic in a pot.
2. Add pork, aji panca, peanuts, and dried potatoes.
3. Pour in water and wine.
4. Simmer until potatoes are tender.
5. Season with salt and pepper.
6. Serve hot. Enjoy the unique flavors of Peruvian carapulcra!

Substitutions

- Use beef or chicken.

4 servings

340 cal

60 mins

Peruvian Adobo

Adobo is a flavorsome Peruvian pork stew, slow-cooked with a blend of spices, garlic, and chicha de jora.

Ingredients:

- 1 lb pork loin
- 1/4 cup aji panca paste
- 1/4 cup aji mirasol paste
- 1/4 cup chopped onions
- 2 garlic cloves
- 1/2 cup chicha de jora (Peruvian corn beer)
- 1/4 cup vinegar
- 1/4 cup white wine
- 8 cups water
- Salt and pepper

Directions

1. Sauté onion and garlic in a pot.
2. Add pork, aji panca, aji mirasol, chicha de jora, vinegar, and wine.
3. Pour in water.
4. Simmer until pork is tender.
5. Season with salt and pepper.
6. Serve hot. Enjoy the rich and aromatic Peruvian adobo!

Substitutions

- Use beef or chicken.

4 servings

360 cal

75 mins

Normal

Peruvian Estofado (Beef Stew)

Estofado is a hearty beef stew with a rich tomato-based sauce, potatoes, and a medley of vegetables.

Ingredients:

- 1 lb beef stew meat
- 1/2 cup diced potatoes
- 1/2 cup diced carrots
- 1/2 cup diced bell peppers
- 1/4 cup chopped onions
- 2 garlic cloves
- 1/2 cup tomato paste
- 1/4 cup white wine
- 8 cups beef broth
- Salt and pepper

Directions

1. Sauté onion and garlic in a pot.
2. Add beef, potatoes, carrots, bell peppers, and tomato paste.
3. Pour in wine and broth.
4. Simmer until beef is tender.
5. Season with salt and pepper.
6. Serve hot. Enjoy the hearty and flavorful Peruvian estofado!

Substitutions

- Use lamb or pork.

Chapter 4:
Main Courses - Meat

4
servings

380 cal

30 mins

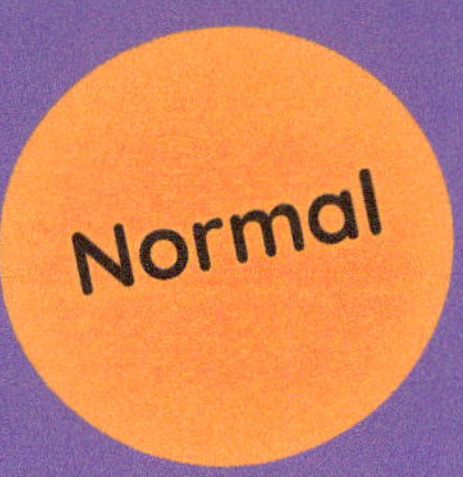

Lomo Saltado (Beef Stir-Fry)

Lomo Saltado is a classic Peruvian stir-fry with tender strips of beef, onions, tomatoes, and French fries.

Ingredients:

- 1 lb beef sirloin
- 2 cups French fries
- 1/2 cup red onion
- 1/2 cup tomatoes
- 1/4 cup yellow chili peppers
- 2 garlic cloves
- 1/4 cup soy sauce
- 2 tbsp vinegar
- Salt and pepper

Directions

1. Heat oil in a pan, add garlic and beef strips.
2. Sauté until beef is browned.
3. Add onions, tomatoes, and chili peppers.
4. Stir in soy sauce and vinegar.
5. Season with salt and pepper.
6. Serve over French fries. Enjoy the sizzling Lomo Saltado!

Substitutions

- Use chicken or tofu.

4 servings | 340 cal | 75 mins

Normal

Seco de Res (Beef Stew)

Seco de Res is a comforting Peruvian beef stew, slow-cooked with cilantro, beer, and served with beans and rice.

Ingredients:

- 1 lb beef stew meat
- 1/2 cup diced onions
- 1/2 cup diced tomatoes
- 1/4 cup cilantro
- 2 garlic cloves
- 1/4 cup beer
- 1/4 cup vegetable oil
- 2 cups cooked canary beans
- 2 cups cooked rice
- Salt and pepper

Directions

1. Sauté onions and garlic in oil.
2. Add beef and brown.
3. Stir in tomatoes, cilantro, beer, salt, and pepper.
4. Simmer until beef is tender.
5. Serve with beans and rice. Enjoy the comforting Seco de Res!

Substitutions

- Use lamb or pork.

4
servings

380 cal

90 mins

Pollo a la Brasa (Rotisserie Chicken)

Normal

Pollo a la Brasa is a beloved Peruvian rotisserie chicken, marinated in a flavorful spice blend and roasted to perfection.

Ingredients:

- 1 whole chicken
- 2 tbsp soy sauce
- 2 tbsp vegetable oil
- 1 tbsp paprika
- 1 tsp cumin
- 1 tsp oregano
- 4 garlic cloves
- 1 lime
- Salt and pepper

Directions

1. Mix soy sauce, oil, paprika, cumin, oregano, garlic, lime juice, salt, and pepper.
2. Rub the chicken with the marinade.
3. Refrigerate for at least 4 hours.
4. Roast the chicken until golden and cooked through.
5. Slice and serve. Enjoy the flavorful Pollo a la Brasa!

Substitutions

- Use chicken parts.

4 servings

320 cal

60 mins

Aji de Gallina (Chicken Stew)

Aji de Gallina is a creamy Peruvian chicken stew with a mildly spicy yellow chili sauce, served over rice.

Ingredients:

- 1 lb chicken pieces
- 1/2 cup diced onions
- 1/4 cup yellow chili pepper paste
- 2 garlic cloves
- 2 cups chicken broth
- 1/2 cup evaporated milk
- 1/4 cup grated parmesan cheese
- 4 cups cooked rice
- Salt and pepper

Directions

1. Sauté onions and garlic until soft.
2. Add chicken and brown.
3. Stir in yellow chili paste.
4. Pour in chicken broth and simmer.
5. Add milk and cheese, stirring until creamy.
6. Season with salt and pepper.
7. Serve over rice. Enjoy the creamy Aji de Gallina!

Substitutions

- Use tofu or mushrooms.

4 servings

400 cal

90 mins

Normal

Carapulcra con Sopa Seca

Carapulcra con Sopa Seca is a traditional Peruvian dish, featuring dried potatoes stewed with pork, served with noodles.

Ingredients:

- 1/2 lb pork loin
- 1/2 cup dried potatoes
- 1/4 cup aji panca paste
- 1/4 cup peanuts
- 1/4 cup chopped onions
- 2 garlic cloves
- 1/2 cup white wine
- 8 cups water
- 1/2 lb noodles
- Salt and pepper

Directions

1. Sauté onions and garlic until soft.
2. Add pork and brown.
3. Stir in aji panca, peanuts, and dried potatoes.
4. Pour in white wine and water.
5. Simmer until potatoes are tender.
6. Cook noodles separately.
7. Serve the stew with noodles. Enjoy Carapulcra con Sopa Seca!

Substitutions

- Use beef or chicken.

4 servings

360 cal

60 mins

Peruvian Beef Hearts with Potatoes

This dish features marinated beef hearts, skewered and grilled to perfection, served with potatoes.

Ingredients:

- 1 lb beef hearts
- 1/4 cup aji panca paste
- 1/4 cup vinegar
- 1/4 cup vegetable oil
- 1/4 cup chopped onions
- 2 garlic cloves
- 4 large potatoes
- Salt and pepper

Directions

1. Mix aji panca, vinegar, oil, onions, and garlic for marinade.
2. Cut beef hearts into chunks, marinate.
3. Thread onto skewers and grill until cooked.
4. Boil and slice potatoes, season with salt and pepper.
5. Serve together. Enjoy the flavorful Peruvian Beef Hearts with Potatoes!

Substitutions

- Use beef sirloin.

4 skewers

320 cal

40 mins

Anticuchos (Grilled Beef Heart)

Anticuchos are marinated beef heart skewers, a popular street food delicacy in Peru, rich in flavor.

Ingredients:

- 1 lb beef heart
- 1/4 cup aji panca paste
- 2 garlic cloves
- 1/4 cup vinegar
- 2 tbsp vegetable oil
- Skewers
- Salt and pepper

Directions

1. Cut beef heart into chunks.
2. Mix aji panca, garlic, vinegar, and oil for marinade.
3. Thread onto skewers.
4. Grill until cooked, basting with marinade.
5. Season with salt and pepper.
6. Serve the delicious Anticuchos!

Substitutions

- Use beef sirloin.

4 servings | 400 cal | 60 mins

Tacu Tacu with Lomo Saltado

Tacu Tacu is a Peruvian dish made with rice and beans, served with a side of Lomo Saltado for a hearty meal.

Ingredients:

- 2 cups cooked rice
- 1 cup cooked canary beans
- 1/2 cup diced onions
- 2 garlic cloves
- 1 lb beef sirloin strips
- 1/2 cup red onion
- 1/2 cup tomatoes
- 1/4 cup yellow chili peppers
- 2 garlic cloves
- 1/4 cup soy sauce
- 2 tbsp vinegar
- Salt and pepper

Directions

1. Sauté onions and garlic until soft.
2. Stir in rice and beans, cook until crispy.
3. In a separate pan, sauté beef strips with garlic, onions, tomatoes, and chili peppers.
4. Add soy sauce and vinegar, season with salt and pepper.
5. Serve Tacu Tacu with Lomo Saltado on the side. Enjoy the satisfying combination!

Substitutions

- Use chicken or tofu.

4 servings

340 cal

75 mins

Chanfainita (Beef and Potato Stew)

Chanfainita is a Peruvian stew made with beef, potatoes, and peanuts, offering a unique blend of flavors.

Ingredients:

- 1 lb beef stew meat
- 1/2 cup diced potatoes
- 1/4 cup peanuts
- 1/4 cup diced onions
- 2 garlic cloves
- 1/2 cup beef broth
- 1/2 cup evaporated milk
- 2 eggs
- Salt and pepper

Directions

1. Sauté onions and garlic until soft.
2. Add beef and brown.
3. Stir in potatoes, peanuts, broth, and milk.
4. Simmer until potatoes are tender.
5. Beat eggs and add to the stew, stirring until creamy.
6. Season with salt and pepper.
7. Serve the unique Chanfainita stew!

Substitutions

- Use lamb or pork.

4 servings

400 cal

120 mins

Pachamanca (Andean Meat and Potato Bake)

Pachamanca is a traditional Andean dish featuring meat, potatoes, and vegetables, cooked underground for a smoky flavor.

Ingredients:

- 1 lb beef or lamb
- 1/2 lb pork
- 4 large potatoes
- 4 ears of corn
- 4 sweet potatoes
- 4 fava bean pods
- Banana leaves
- Maras salt
- Black mint leaves (huacatay)

Directions

1. Create layers of meat, potatoes, corn, sweet potatoes, and fava beans on banana leaves.
2. Season with Maras salt and huacatay.
3. Wrap tightly in the leaves.
4. Dig a pit, place stones and wood, and light a fire.
5. Cover with dirt and let it cook for 2 hours.
6. Unearth the Pachamanca and enjoy the smoky flavors of the Andes!

Substitutions

- Use chicken or vegetables.

Chapter 5:
Main Courses - Seafood

4 servings | 260 cal | 30 mins

Normal

Peruvian Ceviche

Ingredients:

- 1 lb white fish or shrimp
- 1/2 cup lime juice
- 1/4 cup lemon juice
- 1/4 cup orange juice
- 1/2 cup red onion
- 1/4 cup cilantro
- 1/4 cup corn kernels
- 1/4 cup sweet potato
- Salt and pepper

Peruvian Ceviche is a refreshing seafood dish featuring fresh fish or shrimp, marinated in citrus juices and served with onions and sweet potato.

Directions

1. Cut fish or shrimp into bite-sized pieces.
2. Mix lime, lemon, and orange juices, pour over seafood.
3. Add onions, cilantro, and season with salt and pepper.
4. Refrigerate for 20 mins.
5. Serve with corn and sweet potato. Enjoy the zesty Peruvian Ceviche!

Substitutions

- Use cooked octopus or scallops.

4 servings

400 cal

45 mins

Arroz con Mariscos (Seafood Rice)

Arroz con Mariscos is a flavorful Peruvian dish featuring rice cooked with a medley of seafood and spices.

Ingredients:

- 1 cup rice
- 1/2 lb mixed seafood (shrimp, squid, mussels)
- 1/2 cup diced onions
- 1/2 cup diced tomatoes
- 1/4 cup peas
- 2 garlic cloves
- 1/2 cup fish or seafood broth
- 1/4 cup white wine
- 1/4 cup vegetable oil
- 1/2 tsp paprika
- Salt and pepper

Directions

1. Sauté onions and garlic in oil until soft.
2. Stir in rice and paprika, cook until translucent.
3. Add seafood, tomatoes, and peas.
4. Pour in broth and wine, season with salt and pepper.
5. Simmer until seafood is cooked.
6. Serve the aromatic Arroz con Mariscos!

Substitutions

- Use your choice of seafood.

4 servings

260 cal

20 mins

Peruvian Tiradito

Peruvian Tiradito is a delicate dish of thinly sliced fish, similar to ceviche but with a creamy aji amarillo sauce.

Ingredients:

- 1 lb white fish fillets
- 1/4 cup lime juice
- 1/4 cup aji amarillo paste
- 2 garlic cloves
- 1/4 cup vegetable oil
- Salt and pepper

Directions

1. Slice fish thinly and arrange on a plate.
2. Mix lime juice, aji amarillo, garlic, and oil.
3. Pour sauce over the fish.
4. Season with salt and pepper.
5. Serve immediately. Enjoy the delicate Peruvian Tiradito!

Substitutions

- Use cooked shrimp or scallops.

4 servings

320 cal

30 mins

Choros a la Chalaca (Mussels)

Choros a la Chalaca is a popular Peruvian dish featuring mussels topped with salsa criolla, lime, and corn.

Ingredients:

- 2 lbs mussels
- 1/2 cup red onion
- 1/4 cup diced tomatoes
- 1/4 cup cilantro
- 1/4 cup corn kernels
- 1/4 cup lime juice
- Salt and pepper

Directions

1. Steam mussels until they open, discard any unopened ones.
2. Prepare salsa by mixing onions, tomatoes, cilantro, corn, lime juice, salt, and pepper.
3. Top each mussel with salsa.
4. Serve immediately. Enjoy the flavors of Choros a la Chalaca!

Substitutions

- Use clams or oysters.

4 servings

320 cal

45 mins

Sudado de Pescado (Fish Stew)

Sudado de Pescado is a comforting Peruvian fish stew with tomatoes, onions, and aji panca, served over rice.

Ingredients:

- 1 lb white fish fillets
- 1/2 cup diced onions
- 1/2 cup diced tomatoes
- 1/4 cup aji panca paste
- 2 garlic cloves
- 2 cups fish broth
- 1/4 cup white wine
- 1/4 cup vegetable oil
- 1/2 cup peas
- Salt and pepper

Directions

1. Sauté onions and garlic in oil until soft.
2. Stir in aji panca and tomatoes, cook for a few minutes.
3. Add fish, broth, wine, peas, salt, and pepper.
4. Simmer until fish is cooked.
5. Serve over rice. Enjoy the comforting Sudado de Pescado!

Substitutions

- Use seafood mix or shrimp.

4 servings

400 cal

60 mins

Jalea (Fried Seafood Platter)

Jalea is a delightful Peruvian dish featuring a crispy fried seafood platter, served with yuca and salsa criolla.

Ingredients:

- 1/2 lb mixed seafood (shrimp, squid, fish)
- 1/2 cup all-purpose flour
- 1/4 cup cornstarch
- 1/2 cup cold water
- 1/2 cup yuca (cassava) fries
- 1/2 cup salsa criolla (onion and lime salsa)
- Oil for frying
- Salt and pepper

Directions

1. Mix flour, cornstarch, cold water, salt, and pepper to create a batter.
2. Heat oil for frying.
3. Dip seafood in batter and fry until golden.
4. Serve with yuca fries and salsa criolla. Enjoy the crispy Jalea!

Substitutions

- Use your choice of seafood.

4 servings | 280 cal | 60 mins

Peruvian Grilled Octopus (Pulpo)

Pulpo a la Parrilla is a tender grilled octopus dish, seasoned with aji panca and served with potatoes.

Ingredients:

- 2 lbs octopus tentacles
- 1/4 cup aji panca paste
- 1/4 cup lime juice
- 2 garlic cloves
- 1/4 cup olive oil
- 4 large potatoes
- Salt and pepper

Directions

1. Mix aji panca, lime juice, garlic, and olive oil for marinade.
2. Grill octopus until charred and tender.
3. Boil and slice potatoes, season with salt and pepper.
4. Serve octopus over potatoes. Enjoy the grilled Pulpo a la Parrilla!

Substitutions

- Use squid or cuttlefish.

4 servings

340 cal

30 mins

Peruvian Shrimp Stir-Fry (Saltado)

Saltado de Camarones is a quick and flavorful Peruvian shrimp stir-fry with onions, tomatoes, and soy sauce.

Ingredients:

- 1 lb shrimp
- 1/2 cup red onion
- 1/2 cup tomatoes
- 1/4 cup soy sauce
- 2 garlic cloves
- 2 cups cooked rice
- 1/4 cup vegetable oil
- Salt and pepper

Directions

1. Heat oil in a pan, add garlic and shrimp, sauté until pink.
2. Add onions, tomatoes, and soy sauce, stir-fry briefly.
3. Season with salt and pepper.
4. Serve over cooked rice. Enjoy the flavorful Saltado de Camarones!

Substitutions

- Use chicken or tofu.

4 servings | 280 cal | 30 mins

Normal

Peruvian Scallop Ceviche (Conchitas)

Conchitas a la Parmesana is a delightful Peruvian scallop ceviche, topped with Parmesan cheese and baked to perfection.

Ingredients:

- 1 lb scallops
- 1/4 cup lime juice
- 1/4 cup white wine
- 1/4 cup grated Parmesan cheese
- 2 garlic cloves
- 1/4 cup butter
- Salt and pepper

Directions

1. Mix lime juice, white wine, garlic, salt, and pepper for marinade.
2. Add scallops and marinate briefly.
3. Place scallops in a baking dish, top with Parmesan cheese and butter.
4. Bake until cheese is bubbly and golden.
5. Serve the cheesy Peruvian Scallop Ceviche!

Substitutions

- Use shrimp or fish.

4 servings

380 cal

60 mins

Peruvian Paella

Peruvian Paella is a fusion of Spanish paella and Peruvian flavors, featuring seafood, chicken, and rice cooked to perfection.

Ingredients:

- 1 cup rice
- 1/2 lb mixed seafood (shrimp, squid, mussels)
- 1/2 lb chicken pieces
- 1/4 cup diced onions
- 1/4 cup diced tomatoes
- 1/4 cup peas
- 2 garlic cloves
- 1/4 cup white wine
- 1/4 cup vegetable oil
- 1/2 tsp paprika
- Salt and pepper

Directions

1. Sauté onions and garlic in oil until soft.
2. Stir in rice and paprika, cook until translucent.
3. Add chicken, seafood, tomatoes, peas, white wine, salt, and pepper.
4. Simmer until rice is cooked and seafood is done.
5. Serve the flavorful Peruvian Paella!

Substitutions

- Use your choice of seafood or meats.

A small favor to ask

My fellow culinary explorers,

In the midst of our journey through the flavors of Peru within the pages of the "Peruvian Comforts Cookbook: Savor Peruvian Flavors - 100+ Authentic Recipes," I'd like to take a moment to discuss something of great importance to us—your thoughts and feedback.

You see, in the world of cookbooks, reviews are a rare treasure. They are like the secret ingredients that transform a dish from good to unforgettable. They are the spice that adds depth and character to our culinary creations.

Reviews, my friends, are hard to come by, especially for a small and passionate publishing team like ours. But you, our cherished readers, have the power to make a difference.

If you've found joy and inspiration in the pages of this cookbook, if the flavors of Peru have danced on your taste buds and if the recipes have graced your table with their authenticity, then I kindly ask for your support.

Please, when you have a moment, return to the app or platform where you acquired this book. There, you'll find a review button waiting for your input. A star rating and a brief sentence sharing your thoughts would mean the world to us. Your review could inspire others to embark on their own culinary adventure through the vibrant and diverse landscape of Peruvian cuisine.

We are a small publishing team, and your reviews are not just numbers to us; they are a lifeline, a source of inspiration, and a testament to our shared love for the culinary arts.

So, let's return to these pages, to the recipes that transport us to Peru, to the flavors that awaken our senses, and to the joy of cooking. And when you're ready, consider leaving a review that will not only touch our hearts but also guide future explorers on their own Peruvian culinary odyssey.

Now, let's delve back into the enchanting world of Peruvian cuisine, where each dish tells a story, and each bite is a celebration of culture and tradition. Thank you for being a part of this journey, and thank you in advance for your reviews. Onward, my fellow adventurers!

Chapter 6:
Main Courses - Vegetarian

4 servings | 340 cal | 75 mins

Quinoa Stuffed Bell Peppers (Rocoto Relleno)

Normal

Rocoto Relleno features bell peppers stuffed with a hearty quinoa and vegetable mixture, baked to perfection.

Ingredients:

- 4 large bell peppers
- 1 cup quinoa
- 2 cups vegetable broth
- 1/2 cup diced onions
- 1/2 cup diced tomatoes
- 1/4 cup peas
- 2 garlic cloves
- 1/4 cup aji panca paste
- 1/4 cup grated cheese
- Salt and pepper

Directions

1. Cut the tops off the bell peppers and remove seeds.
2. Rinse quinoa and cook in vegetable broth until tender.
3. Sauté onions, garlic, and aji panca paste until fragrant.
4. Stir in tomatoes, peas, cooked quinoa, salt, and pepper.
5. Stuff bell peppers with the quinoa mixture.
6. Top with grated cheese.
7. Bake until peppers are tender.
8. Serve the flavorful Rocoto Relleno!

Substitutions

- Use rice instead of quinoa.

4 servings | 320 cal | 30 mins

Papa a la Huancaína (Potatoes in Cheese Sauce)

Papa a la Huancaína is a classic Peruvian dish featuring boiled potatoes smothered in a creamy cheese sauce.

Ingredients:

- 4 large potatoes
- 1 cup queso fresco (fresh cheese)
- 1/4 cup aji amarillo paste
- 2 garlic cloves
- 1/2 cup evaporated milk
- 2 soda crackers
- 1/4 cup vegetable oil
- Lettuce leaves
- Black olives
- Hard-boiled eggs
- Saltine crackers
- Salt and pepper

Directions

1. Boil potatoes until tender, peel, and slice.
2. Blend queso fresco, aji amarillo, garlic, evaporated milk, and soda crackers until creamy.
3. Season with salt and pepper.
4. Serve potatoes on lettuce leaves, drizzle with cheese sauce.
5. Garnish with olives and sliced hard-boiled eggs.
6. Serve with saltine crackers. Enjoy Papa a la Huancaína!

Substitutions

- Use feta or cream cheese if queso fresco is unavailable.

4 servings | 360 cal | 60 mins

Tacu Tacu with Salsa Criolla

Tacu Tacu is a Peruvian dish made with rice and beans, served with a zesty Salsa Criolla on top.

Ingredients:

- 2 cups cooked rice
- 1 cup cooked canary beans
- 1/2 cup diced onions
- 2 garlic cloves
- 1/4 cup aji amarillo paste
- 1/4 cup vegetable oil
- Salt and pepper
- 1/2 cup Salsa Criolla (onion and lime salsa)

Directions

1. Sauté onions and garlic in oil until soft.
2. Stir in aji amarillo paste, cooked rice, and beans.
3. Mash mixture and cook until crispy on the bottom.
4. Flip and cook until crispy on the other side.
5. Season with salt and pepper.
6. Serve with Salsa Criolla on top. Enjoy Tacu Tacu!

Substitutions

- Use black beans or your choice of beans.

4 servings | 340 cal | 45 mins

Ocopa Arequipeña

Ocopa Arequipeña is a traditional Peruvian dish featuring boiled potatoes covered in a creamy peanut sauce.

Ingredients:

- 4 large potatoes
- 1/2 cup roasted peanuts
- 1/4 cup aji amarillo paste
- 2 garlic cloves
- 1/2 cup evaporated milk
- 1/4 cup vegetable oil
- 2 hard-boiled eggs
- Black olives
- Salt and pepper

Directions

1. Boil potatoes until tender, peel, and slice.
2. Blend peanuts, aji amarillo, garlic, evaporated milk, and oil until creamy.
3. Season with salt and pepper.
4. Serve potatoes with peanut sauce on top.
5. Garnish with sliced hard-boiled eggs and black olives.
6. Enjoy the creamy Ocopa Arequipeña!

Substitutions

- Use almond or cashew butter if peanuts are not preferred.

4
servings

300 cal

30 mins

Peruvian Mushroom Stir-Fry

Peruvian Mushroom Stir-Fry is a vegetarian delight featuring sautéed mushrooms, tomatoes, and aji amarillo.

Ingredients:

- 1 lb mushrooms
- 1/2 cup diced tomatoes
- 1/4 cup diced onions
- 2 garlic cloves
- 1/4 cup aji amarillo paste
- 1/4 cup vegetable broth
- 1/4 cup vegetable oil
- Salt and pepper
- Chopped cilantro for garnish

Directions

1. Heat oil in a pan, sauté onions and garlic until soft.
2. Add mushrooms and cook until browned.
3. Stir in tomatoes, aji amarillo paste, and vegetable broth.
4. Season with salt and pepper.
5. Cook until mushrooms are tender.
6. Garnish with chopped cilantro.
7. Serve the savory Peruvian Mushroom Stir-Fry!

Substitutions

- Use your favorite vegetables or tofu for a variation.

4 servings

380 cal

45 mins

Quinotto (Quinoa Risotto)

Quinotto is a Peruvian twist on classic risotto, made with quinoa cooked in a creamy aji amarillo sauce.

Ingredients:

- 1 cup quinoa
- 1/2 cup diced onions
- 2 garlic cloves
- 1/4 cup aji amarillo paste
- 1/4 cup vegetable broth
- 1/2 cup grated Parmesan cheese
- 1/4 cup heavy cream
- 1/4 cup vegetable oil
- Salt and pepper
- Chopped parsley for garnish

Directions

1. Sauté onions and garlic in oil until soft.
2. Stir in quinoa and aji amarillo paste, cook for a few minutes.
3. Add vegetable broth, salt, and pepper.
4. Simmer until quinoa is tender.
5. Stir in Parmesan cheese, heavy cream, and cook until creamy.
6. Garnish with chopped parsley.
7. Serve the delightful Quinotto!

Substitutions

- Use vegetable broth for a vegetarian version.

4 servings | 360 cal | 30 mins

Peruvian Stir-Fried Rice (Arroz Chaufa)

Arroz Chaufa is a Peruvian stir-fried rice dish loaded with vegetables and your choice of protein.

Ingredients:

- 2 cups cooked rice
- 1/2 cup diced cooked chicken or tofu
- 1/4 cup diced onions
- 1/4 cup diced bell peppers
- 1/4 cup peas
- 2 garlic cloves
- 2 eggs
- 1/4 cup soy sauce
- 1/4 cup vegetable oil
- Salt and pepper

Directions

1. Heat oil in a pan, sauté onions and garlic until soft.
2. Add diced chicken or tofu, cook until browned.
3. Push the protein to the side and scramble eggs in the pan.
4. Stir in cooked rice, bell peppers, peas, and soy sauce.
5. Cook until heated through.
6. Season with salt and pepper.
7. Serve the savory Arroz Chaufa!

Substitutions

- Use shrimp or beef for a meaty version.

4
servings

320 cal

30 mins

Peruvian Quinoa Salad

Peruvian Quinoa Salad is a refreshing and nutritious dish made with quinoa, veggies, and a zesty lime dressing.

Ingredients:

- 1 cup quinoa
- 1/2 cup diced tomatoes
- 1/2 cup diced cucumbers
- 1/4 cup diced red onion
- 1/4 cup chopped cilantro
- 1/4 cup lime juice
- 1/4 cup olive oil
- Salt and pepper

Directions

1. Rinse quinoa and cook according to package instructions.
2. Let quinoa cool.
3. In a bowl, combine quinoa, tomatoes, cucumbers, red onion, and cilantro.
4. In a separate bowl, whisk together lime juice, olive oil, salt, and pepper to make the dressing.
5. Drizzle dressing over the salad and toss.
6. Serve the refreshing Peruvian Quinoa Salad!

Substitutions

- Add diced avocado or black beans for extra flavor.

4 servings

340 cal

30 mins

Peruvian Stuffed Avocado

Peruvian Stuffed Avocado is a simple yet flavorful dish featuring ripe avocados stuffed with a quinoa and veggie mixture.

Ingredients:

- 2 ripe avocados
- 1 cup cooked quinoa
- 1/2 cup diced tomatoes
- 1/2 cup diced cucumbers
- 1/4 cup diced red onion
- 1/4 cup chopped cilantro
- 1/4 cup lime juice
- 1/4 cup olive oil
- Salt and pepper

Directions

1. Cut avocados in half and remove pits.
2. In a bowl, combine cooked quinoa, tomatoes, cucumbers, red onion, and cilantro.
3. In a separate bowl, whisk together lime juice, olive oil, salt, and pepper to make the dressing.
4. Drizzle dressing over the quinoa mixture and toss.
5. Fill each avocado half with the quinoa mixture.
6. Serve the delightful Peruvian Stuffed Avocado!

Substitutions

- Add crumbled feta or goat cheese for extra creaminess.

4 servings

280 cal

45 mins

Easy

Ajiaco de Papas (Potato Soup)

Ajiaco de Papas is a comforting Peruvian potato soup featuring potatoes, cheese, and a touch of aji amarillo.

Ingredients:

- 4 large potatoes
- 1/2 cup queso fresco (fresh cheese)
- 1/4 cup aji amarillo paste
- 2 garlic cloves
- 1/2 cup evaporated milk
- 1/4 cup vegetable oil
- Salt and pepper

Directions

1. Boil potatoes until tender, peel, and mash them.
2. In a pot, sauté garlic and aji amarillo paste in oil until fragrant.
3. Stir in mashed potatoes and cook for a few minutes.
4. Add queso fresco, evaporated milk, salt, and pepper.
5. Simmer until cheese is melted and soup is creamy.
6. Serve the comforting Ajiaco de Papas!

Substitutions

- Use feta or cream cheese if queso fresco is unavailable.

Chapter 7:
Rice and Grains

4 servings

420 cal

60 mins

Arroz con Pollo (Peruvian Chicken and Rice)

Arroz con Pollo is a classic Peruvian dish featuring tender chicken and rice cooked with vibrant spices and vegetables.

Ingredients:

- 1 lb chicken pieces
- 2 cups rice
- 1/2 cup diced onions
- 1/2 cup diced bell peppers
- 1/4 cup green peas
- 2 garlic cloves
- 1/4 cup aji amarillo paste
- 1/4 cup vegetable oil
- 1/2 cup beer
- 2 cups chicken broth
- 1/2 tsp cumin
- 1/2 tsp paprika
- Salt and pepper
- Chopped cilantro for garnish

Substitutions

- Use vegetable broth for a vegetarian version.

Directions

1. Season chicken with cumin, paprika, salt, and pepper.
2. In a large pot, heat oil and brown chicken on all sides.
3. Remove chicken and set aside.
4. In the same pot, sauté onions, garlic, bell peppers, and aji amarillo paste until soft.
5. Stir in rice and cook for a few minutes.
6. Add beer, chicken broth, green peas, and return chicken to the pot.
7. Simmer until rice is cooked and chicken is tender.
8. Garnish with chopped cilantro.
9. Serve the flavorful Arroz con Pollo!

4 servings

320 cal

30 mins

Easy

Peruvian Quinoa Salad

Peruvian Quinoa Salad is a refreshing and nutritious dish made with quinoa, veggies, and a zesty lime dressing.

Ingredients:

- 1 cup quinoa
- 1/2 cup diced tomatoes
- 1/2 cup diced cucumbers
- 1/4 cup diced red onion
- 1/4 cup chopped cilantro
- 1/4 cup lime juice
- 1/4 cup olive oil
- Salt and pepper

Directions

1. Rinse quinoa and cook according to package instructions.
2. Let quinoa cool.
3. In a bowl, combine quinoa, tomatoes, cucumbers, red onion, and cilantro.
4. In a separate bowl, whisk together lime juice, olive oil, salt, and pepper to make the dressing.
5. Drizzle dressing over the salad and toss.
6. Serve the refreshing Peruvian Quinoa Salad!

Substitutions

- Add diced avocado or black beans for extra flavor.

4 servings | 400 cal | 30 mins

Arroz Chaufa (Peruvian Fried Rice)

Arroz Chaufa is a Peruvian stir-fried rice dish loaded with vegetables and your choice of protein.

Ingredients:

- 2 cups cooked rice
- 1/2 cup diced cooked chicken or tofu
- 1/4 cup diced onions
- 1/4 cup diced bell peppers
- 1/4 cup peas
- 2 garlic cloves
- 2 eggs
- 1/4 cup soy sauce
- 1/4 cup vegetable oil
- Salt and pepper

Directions

1. Heat oil in a pan, sauté onions and garlic until soft.
2. Add diced chicken or tofu, cook until browned.
3. Push the protein to the side and scramble eggs in the pan.
4. Stir in cooked rice, bell peppers, peas, and soy sauce.
5. Cook until heated through.
6. Season with salt and pepper.
7. Serve the savory Arroz Chaufa!

Substitutions

- Use shrimp or beef for a meaty version.

4 servings

400 cal

60 mins

Tacu Tacu

Tacu Tacu is a Peruvian dish made with rice and beans, served with a zesty Salsa Criolla on top.

Ingredients:

- 2 cups cooked rice
- 1 cup cooked canary beans
- 1/2 cup diced onions
- 2 garlic cloves
- 1/4 cup aji amarillo paste
- 1/4 cup vegetable oil
- Salt and pepper
- 1/2 cup Salsa Criolla (onion and lime salsa)

Directions

1. Sauté onions and garlic in oil until soft.
2. Stir in aji amarillo paste, cooked rice, and beans.
3. Mash mixture and cook until crispy on the bottom.
4. Flip and cook until crispy on the other side.
5. Season with salt and pepper.
6. Serve with Salsa Criolla on top. Enjoy Tacu Tacu!

Substitutions

- Use black beans or your choice of beans.

4 servings

420 cal

45 mins

Peruvian Risotto (Arroz con Mariscos)

Peruvian Risotto is a seafood lover's dream, featuring creamy rice cooked with mixed seafood and aji amarillo.

Ingredients:

- 1 cup rice
- 1/2 lb mixed seafood (shrimp, squid, mussels)
- 1/2 cup diced onions
- 1/4 cup diced tomatoes
- 1/4 cup peas
- 2 garlic cloves
- 1/4 cup white wine
- 1/4 cup vegetable oil
- 1/4 cup aji amarillo paste
- Salt and pepper

Directions

1. Sauté onions and garlic in oil until soft.
2. Stir in rice and cook until translucent.
3. Add mixed seafood, tomatoes, peas, white wine, aji amarillo paste, salt, and pepper.
4. Simmer until rice is cooked and seafood is done.
5. Serve the flavorful Peruvian Risotto!

Substitutions

- Use your choice of seafood or meats.

4 servings

380 cal

45 mins

Normal

Peruvian Fried Quinoa (Quinotto)

Quinotto is a Peruvian twist on classic risotto, made with quinoa cooked in a creamy aji amarillo sauce.

Ingredients:

- 1 cup quinoa
- 1/2 cup diced onions
- 2 garlic cloves
- 1/4 cup aji amarillo paste
- 1/4 cup vegetable broth
- 1/2 cup grated Parmesan cheese
- 1/4 cup heavy cream
- 1/4 cup vegetable oil
- Salt and pepper
- Chopped parsley for garnish

Directions

1. Sauté onions and garlic in oil until soft.
2. Stir in quinoa and aji amarillo paste, cook for a few minutes.
3. Add vegetable broth, salt, and pepper.
4. Simmer until quinoa is tender.
5. Stir in Parmesan cheese, heavy cream, and cook until creamy.
6. Garnish with chopped parsley.
7. Serve the delightful Quinotto!

Substitutions

- Use vegetable broth for a vegetarian version.

4 servings

280 cal

30 mins

Easy

Peruvian Corn Salad (Solterito)

Solterito is a Peruvian corn salad featuring corn, beans, cheese, and veggies dressed in a zesty vinaigrette.

Ingredients:

- 2 cups cooked corn kernels
- 1 cup cooked canary beans
- 1/2 cup diced queso fresco (fresh cheese)
- 1/4 cup diced red onion
- 1/4 cup diced tomatoes
- 1/4 cup diced rocoto or red bell pepper
- 2 hard-boiled eggs
- Black olives
- Chopped cilantro
- Salt and pepper
- 1/4 cup lime juice
- 1/4 cup olive oil

Directions

1. In a bowl, combine corn, canary beans, queso fresco, red onion, tomatoes, and rocoto or red bell pepper.
2. Slice hard-boiled eggs and add to the salad.
3. Garnish with black olives and chopped cilantro.
4. In a separate bowl, whisk together lime juice, olive oil, salt, and pepper to make the dressing.
5. Drizzle dressing over the salad and toss.
6. Serve the vibrant Peruvian Corn Salad!

Substitutions

- Use feta or mozzarella if queso fresco is unavailable.

4 servings

340 cal

45 mins

Peruvian Beans (Tacu Tacu)

Tacu Tacu is a Peruvian dish made with rice and beans, served with a zesty Salsa Criolla on top.

Ingredients:

- 2 cups cooked rice
- 1 cup cooked canary beans
- 1/2 cup diced onions
- 2 garlic cloves
- 1/4 cup aji amarillo paste
- 1/4 cup vegetable oil
- Salt and pepper
- 1/2 cup Salsa Criolla (onion and lime salsa)

Directions

1. Sauté onions and garlic in oil until soft.
2. Stir in aji amarillo paste, cooked rice, and beans.
3. Mash mixture and cook until crispy on the bottom.
4. Flip and cook until crispy on the other side.
5. Season with salt and pepper.
6. Serve with Salsa Criolla on top. Enjoy Tacu Tacu!

Substitutions

- Use black beans or your choice of beans.

4 servings | 280 cal | 60 mins

Peruvian Rice Pudding (Arroz con Leche)

Arroz con Leche is a comforting Peruvian rice pudding flavored with cinnamon and raisins.

Ingredients:

- 1 cup rice
- 1/2 cup raisins
- 4 cups milk
- 1 cup sugar
- 1 cinnamon stick
- 1/4 tsp ground cinnamon
- 1/4 tsp vanilla extract

Directions

1. Rinse rice and combine with milk, sugar, and cinnamon stick in a pot.
2. Cook over low heat, stirring constantly, until rice is tender and mixture thickens.
3. Stir in raisins, ground cinnamon, and vanilla extract.
4. Cook for a few more minutes until raisins plump up.
5. Remove from heat and let it cool slightly.
6. Serve warm or chilled. Enjoy the comforting Arroz con Leche!

Substitutions

- Add a touch of nutmeg or cardamom for extra flavor.

4 servings

360 cal

60 mins

Peruvian Stuffed Potatoes (Papas Rellenas)

Papas Rellenas are flavorful Peruvian stuffed potatoes filled with seasoned ground beef or other fillings.

Ingredients:

- 4 large potatoes
- 1/2 lb ground beef
- 1/4 cup diced onions
- 2 garlic cloves
- 1/4 cup diced tomatoes
- 1/4 cup diced bell peppers
- 2 hard-boiled eggs
- Pitted black olives
- Raisins
- Cumin
- Paprika
- Salt and pepper
- Vegetable oil for frying

Substitutions

- Use vegetarian filling for a meat-free version.

Directions

1. Boil potatoes until tender, peel, and mash them.
2. In a pan, sauté onions and garlic in oil until soft.
3. Add ground beef, tomatoes, bell peppers, and season with cumin, paprika, salt, and pepper.
4. Cook until beef is browned.
5. Shape mashed potatoes into balls and flatten into discs.
6. Place a spoonful of the beef mixture, half a hard-boiled egg, olives, and raisins in the center of each potato disc.
7. Close and seal the potato, forming a ball.
8. Heat oil in a pan and fry the stuffed potatoes until golden brown.
9. Drain excess oil on paper towels.
10. Serve the delicious Papas Rellenas!

Chapter 8:
Breads and Pastries

2 loaves

220 cal

180 mins

Peruvian Bread (Pan Peruano)

Pan Peruano is a traditional Peruvian bread with a crisp crust and soft interior, perfect with butter or jam.

Ingredients:

- 4 cups bread flour
- 2 tsp salt
- 1 tsp sugar
- 1 packet active dry yeast
- 1 1/2 cups warm water
- Vegetable oil (for greasing)
- Cornmeal (for dusting)

Directions

1. In a bowl, combine warm water, sugar, and yeast. Let it sit for 5-10 minutes until foamy.
2. In a large mixing bowl, combine flour and salt.
3. Pour in the yeast mixture and knead until the dough is smooth and elastic.
4. Place the dough in a greased bowl, cover with a damp cloth, and let it rise for about 1 hour or until doubled in size.
5. Preheat your oven to 425°F (220°C).
6. Punch down the dough and divide it into two portions.
7. Shape each portion into a round loaf and place them on a baking sheet dusted with cornmeal.
8. Let the loaves rise for another 30 minutes.
9. Make shallow cuts on the surface of the loaves.
10. Bake in the preheated oven for 25-30 minutes or until the bread is golden brown and sounds hollow when tapped on the bottom.
11. Let the bread cool before slicing and serving. Enjoy your homemade Pan Peruano!

Substitutions

- All-purpose flour can be used if bread flour is unavailable.

6 servings

320 cal

120 mins

Peruvian Stuffed Bread (Pan con Chicharrón)

Easy

Pan con Chicharrón is a delicious Peruvian sandwich filled with crispy pork and salsa criolla.

Ingredients:

- 6 small crusty bread rolls
- 2 cups cooked chicharrón (crispy pork)
- 1 cup Salsa Criolla (onion and lime salsa)
- Aji amarillo sauce (optional)
- Lettuce leaves
- Sliced sweet potato (optional)
- Salt and pepper

Directions

1. If you have leftover chicharrón, reheat it until crispy.
2. Slice the bread rolls in half, but not all the way through.
3. Spread aji amarillo sauce (if using) on the inside of the rolls.
4. Fill each roll with a generous amount of crispy chicharrón.
5. Top with Salsa Criolla, lettuce leaves, and sliced sweet potato if desired.
6. Season with salt and pepper.
7. Close the sandwiches and serve immediately.

Enjoy the flavorful Pan con Chicharrón!

Substitutions

- Use roast pork or shredded chicken as an alternative to chicharrón.

8 tamales

290 cal

240 mins

Peruvian Tamales

Peruvian Tamales are a traditional dish made of seasoned masa dough filled with meat, olives, and more.

Ingredients:

- 2 cups masa harina (corn dough)
- 1 cup chicken or pork broth
- 1/2 cup vegetable oil
- 1/4 cup aji amarillo paste
- 1 tsp salt
- 1/2 tsp cumin
- 1/2 tsp paprika
- 8 banana leaves (10x10 inches each, softened)
- 1 lb cooked and shredded chicken or pork
- 1/2 cup sliced black olives
- 4 hard-boiled eggs, quartered
- 1/2 cup raisins
- 8 small pieces of red bell pepper
- Butcher's twine or kitchen string

Substitutions

- Banana leaves can be substituted with corn husks.

Directions

1. In a large mixing bowl, combine masa harina, chicken or pork broth, vegetable oil, aji amarillo paste, salt, cumin, and paprika. Mix until you have a smooth dough.
2. To assemble each tamal, place a softened banana leaf on a clean surface.
3. Spread a small amount of masa dough in the center of the banana leaf, forming a square.
4. Place a portion of shredded meat, olives, a piece of hard-boiled egg, raisins, and a slice of red bell pepper on top of the masa square.
5. Carefully fold the banana leaf over the filling, then fold in the sides to create a rectangular package. Tie it closed with butcher's twine or kitchen string.
6. Repeat this process for the remaining tamales.
7. Place the tamales upright in a large steamer pot.
8. Steam over medium heat for about 2-3 hours, adding more water as needed.
9. To check for doneness, remove one tamal and let it cool for a few minutes. If it easily pulls away from the banana leaf, it's ready.
10. Serve the hot tamales and enjoy this Peruvian delight!

12 empanadas

250 cal

90 mins

Peruvian Empanadas

Peruvian Empanadas are savory pastry pockets filled with seasoned ground beef, olives, and raisins.

Ingredients:

- 2 cups all-purpose flour
- 1/2 tsp salt
- 1/2 cup unsalted butter, cold and cubed
- 1/2 cup cold water
- 1 lb ground beef
- 1/2 cup diced onions
- 2 garlic cloves
- 1/2 cup diced tomatoes
- 1/4 cup sliced black olives
- 1/4 cup raisins
- 1 hard-boiled egg, chopped
- 1 tsp ground cumin
- 1/2 tsp paprika
- Salt and pepper
- Vegetable oil (for frying)

Substitutions

- You can use pre-made empanada dough for a quicker preparation.

Directions

1. In a large mixing bowl, combine flour and salt.
2. Add cold, cubed butter and use a pastry cutter or your fingers to work the butter into the flour until it resembles coarse crumbs.
3. Gradually add cold water and mix until the dough comes together. Shape it into a ball, wrap in plastic wrap, and refrigerate for 30 minutes.
4. While the dough chills, prepare the filling. In a pan, sauté onions and garlic until softened. Add ground beef and cook until browned. Stir in diced tomatoes, olives, raisins, chopped hard-boiled egg, cumin, paprika, salt, and pepper. Cook until well combined. Let the filling cool.
5. Preheat vegetable oil in a deep frying pan or skillet.
6. Roll out the chilled dough on a floured surface to about 1/8-inch thickness.
7. Cut out rounds using a round cutter or a glass.
8. Place a spoonful of the meat filling in the center of each round.
9. Fold the dough over to create a half-moon shape and press the edges to seal.
10. Use a fork to crimp the edges for a decorative seal.
11. Fry the empanadas in batches until golden brown and crispy, about 3-4 minutes per side.
12. Drain on paper towels.
13. Serve the hot Peruvian Empanadas and enjoy!

16 tequeño s

200 cal

60 mins

Peruvian Tequeños

Peruvian Tequeños are cheese-filled breadsticks wrapped in crispy bacon, perfect for snacking.

Ingredients:

- 16 breadsticks or bread dough strips
- 8 slices of bacon, halved lengthwise
- 8 oz queso fresco or mozzarella cheese, cut into small sticks
- Vegetable oil (for frying)
- Toothpicks

Directions

1. Preheat vegetable oil in a deep frying pan or skillet.
2. Wrap each breadstick or dough strip with a piece of halved bacon, securing it with a toothpick.
3. Fry the bacon-wrapped breadsticks until the bacon is crispy and the bread is golden brown.
4. Drain on paper towels.
5. Serve the hot Peruvian Tequeños as a delicious snack or appetizer! Enjoy!

Substitutions

- You can use puff pastry instead of bread dough for a flakier texture.

12 donuts

280 cal

120 mins

Peruvian Sweet Potato Donuts (Picarones)

Picarones are sweet potato donuts drizzled with fig syrup, a beloved Peruvian dessert.

Ingredients:

- 1 lb sweet potatoes, peeled and cubed
- 1/2 cup pumpkin puree
- 1 packet active dry yeast
- 1/4 cup warm water
- 3 cups all-purpose flour
- 1/4 cup granulated sugar
- 1/2 tsp salt
- 1/2 tsp anise seeds
- Vegetable oil (for frying)
- Fig syrup (chancaca syrup) for drizzling

Directions

1. Dissolve yeast in warm water and let it sit for 5-10 minutes until foamy.
2. In a pot, boil sweet potatoes until tender, then mash them.
3. In a large mixing bowl, combine mashed sweet potatoes, pumpkin puree, dissolved yeast, flour, sugar, salt, and anise seeds. Mix until you have a smooth dough.
4. Cover the dough and let it rise for about 1 hour or until doubled in size.
5. Preheat vegetable oil in a deep frying pan or skillet.
6. Wet your hands and grab a portion of dough, then form it into a ring shape with a hole in the center (like a donut).
7. Carefully place the picarones in the hot oil and fry until they're golden brown on both sides.
8. Remove the picarones from the oil and drain them on paper towels.
9. Drizzle the warm picarones with fig syrup (chancaca syrup) before serving.
10. Enjoy the sweet and fragrant Peruvian Picarones!

Substitutions

- Use maple syrup or honey as an alternative to fig syrup.

24 alfajores | 180 cal | 60 mins

Normal

Peruvian Alfajores

Peruvian Alfajores are delicate sandwich cookies filled with dulce de leche and dusted with powdered sugar.

Ingredients:

- 1 1/2 cups all-purpose flour
- 1/2 cup cornstarch
- 1/2 cup powdered sugar
- 1/4 tsp salt
- 1 cup unsalted butter, softened
- 1 tsp vanilla extract
- Dulce de leche (for filling)
- Powdered sugar (for dusting)

Directions

1. In a bowl, sift together flour, cornstarch, powdered sugar, and salt.
2. In another bowl, cream together softened butter and vanilla extract until smooth and fluffy.
3. Gradually add the dry ingredients to the butter mixture and mix until a soft dough forms.
4. Shape the dough into a ball, wrap it in plastic wrap, and refrigerate for 30 minutes.
5. Preheat your oven to 350°F (175°C).
6. Roll out the chilled dough on a floured surface to about 1/4-inch thickness.
7. Use a cookie cutter to cut out rounds or desired shapes.
8. Place the cookies on a baking sheet lined with parchment paper.
9. Bake for 10-12 minutes or until the edges are lightly golden.
10. Let the cookies cool completely.
11. Spread dulce de leche on the bottom side of one cookie and sandwich it with another cookie.
12. Dust the alfajores with powdered sugar.
13. Enjoy these delightful Peruvian Alfajores with a cup of coffee or tea!

Substitutions

- You can add shredded coconut to the dulce de leche for extra flavor.

12 servings

260 cal

150 mins

Peruvian Chocolate Bread (Pan con Chocolate)

Pan con Chocolate is a sweet Peruvian bread studded with chocolate chips, perfect for breakfast or dessert.

Ingredients:

- 3 1/2 cups all-purpose flour
- 1/2 cup granulated sugar
- 1/2 tsp salt
- 2 tsp active dry yeast
- 1 cup warm milk
- 1/4 cup unsalted butter, melted
- 1 egg
- 1 cup chocolate chips
- Vegetable oil (for greasing)
- Additional chocolate chips for topping (optional)

Directions

1. In a bowl, dissolve yeast in warm milk and let it sit for 5-10 minutes until foamy.
2. In a separate bowl, mix together flour, sugar, and salt.
3. Add melted butter, the yeast mixture, and an egg to the dry ingredients. Stir until a dough forms.
4. Knead the dough for about 10 minutes on a floured surface until it's smooth and elastic.
5. Place the dough in a greased bowl, cover with a damp cloth, and let it rise for about 1 hour or until doubled in size.
6. Preheat your oven to 350°F (175°C).
7. Punch down the dough and knead in chocolate chips.
8. Shape the dough into a loaf or rolls, placing them in a greased baking pan or on a baking sheet.
9. Let the dough rise for another 30 minutes.
10. If desired, sprinkle additional chocolate chips on top.
11. Bake for 25-30 minutes or until the bread is golden brown and sounds hollow when tapped on the bottom.
12. Let the bread cool before slicing and serving.
13. Enjoy your homemade Peruvian Chocolate Bread!

Substitutions

- You can use chocolate chunks instead of chocolate chips.

12 pastries

220 cal

90 mins

Peruvian Guava Pastry (Pastel de Guayaba)

Pastel de Guayaba is a delightful Peruvian pastry filled with guava paste and cream cheese.

Ingredients:

- 1 sheet puff pastry (thawed)
- 1/2 cup guava paste (cut into small pieces)
- 1/2 cup cream cheese
- 1 egg (for egg wash)
- Powdered sugar (for dusting)
- 1/4 cup milk (for glaze)

Directions

1. Preheat your oven to 375°F (190°C).
2. Roll out the thawed puff pastry on a floured surface.
3. Cut the pastry into squares or rectangles, depending on your preference.
4. In the center of each pastry square, place a small amount of guava paste and cream cheese.
5. Fold the pastry over to create a triangle or rectangle shape and press the edges to seal.
6. Beat the egg and use it as an egg wash to brush the tops of the pastries.
7. Place the pastries on a baking sheet lined with parchment paper.
8. Bake for 20-25 minutes or until the pastries are golden brown and puffed up.
9. While the pastries are baking, prepare a glaze by mixing powdered sugar and milk until smooth.
10. Drizzle the glaze over the warm pastries.
11. Allow them to cool slightly before serving.
12. Enjoy the sweet and flaky Peruvian Pastel de Guayaba!

Substitutions

- You can add a sprinkle of cinnamon for extra flavor.

8 servings

240 cal

120 mins

Easy

Peruvian King Kong

Ingredients:

- 1 sheet puff pastry (thawed)
- 1 cup manjar blanco (dulce de leche)
- 1/4 cup powdered sugar (for dusting)
- 1/4 cup milk (for glaze)
- 1/4 cup colorful sprinkles (for decoration, optional)

Substitutions

- You can add chopped nuts or chocolate chips to the filling.

King Kong is a Peruvian dessert made of layers of buttery pastry filled with manjar blanco (dulce de leche).

Directions

1. Preheat your oven to 375°F (190°C).
2. Roll out the thawed puff pastry on a floured surface.
3. Cut the pastry into rectangles or squares, about the size of your palm.
4. Place a spoonful of manjar blanco (dulce de leche) on one pastry piece, then top it with another piece of pastry, creating a sandwich.
5. Seal the edges by pressing them together with a fork.
6. Place the pastries on a baking sheet lined with parchment paper.
7. Beat the egg and use it as an egg wash to brush the tops of the pastries.
8. Bake for 20-25 minutes or until the pastries are golden brown and puffed up.
9. While the pastries are baking, prepare a glaze by mixing powdered sugar and milk until smooth.
10. Drizzle the glaze over the warm pastries.
11. If desired, decorate with colorful sprinkles.
12. Allow the pastries to cool slightly before serving.
13. Enjoy the delightful Peruvian King Kong!

Chapter 9:
Desserts - Cakes and Sweets

12 servings

350 cal

90 mins

Peruvian Tres Leches Cake

Peruvian Tres Leches Cake is a moist sponge cake soaked in three types of milk and topped with whipped cream and strawberries.

Ingredients:

- 1 cup all-purpose flour
- 1 1/2 tsp baking powder
- 1/4 tsp salt
- 1/4 cup unsalted butter, softened
- 1 cup granulated sugar
- 4 large eggs
- 1 tsp vanilla extract
- 1/2 cup whole milk
- 1 can (12 oz) evaporated milk
- 1 can (14 oz) sweetened condensed milk
- 1 cup heavy cream
- 1/4 cup powdered sugar
- Strawberries (for garnish, optional)

Directions

1. Preheat your oven to 350°F (175°C) and grease a 9x13-inch baking dish.
2. In a bowl, whisk together flour, baking powder, and salt.
3. In a separate large mixing bowl, cream together softened butter and granulated sugar until light and fluffy.
4. Beat in the eggs one at a time, then stir in the vanilla extract.
5. Gradually add the dry ingredients to the wet ingredients, alternating with the whole milk, beginning and ending with the dry mixture. Mix until just combined.
6. Pour the batter into the prepared baking dish and smooth the top.
7. Bake for 30-35 minutes or until a toothpick inserted into the center comes out clean.
8. While the cake is still warm, pierce it all over with a fork.
9. In a separate bowl, whisk together the evaporated milk, sweetened condensed milk, and heavy cream.
10. Pour the milk mixture evenly over the warm cake, allowing it to soak in.
11. Refrigerate the cake for at least 4 hours or overnight.
12. Before serving, whip the heavy cream and powdered sugar until stiff peaks form.
13. Spread the whipped cream over the cake and garnish with sliced strawberries if desired.
14. Enjoy the luscious Peruvian Tres Leches Cake!

Substitutions

- You can use coconut milk for a tropical twist.
- Decorate with other fruits like kiwi or peaches for variety.

12 servings

380 cal

90 mins

Peruvian Chocolate Cake (Torta de Chocolate)

Peruvian Chocolate Cake is a decadent dessert made with rich chocolate cake layers and velvety chocolate ganache.

Ingredients:

- 1 3/4 cups all-purpose flour
- 2 cups granulated sugar
- 3/4 cup unsweetened cocoa powder
- 1 1/2 tsp baking powder
- 1 1/2 tsp baking soda
- 1 tsp salt
- 2 large eggs
- 1 cup whole milk
- 1/2 cup vegetable oil
- 2 tsp vanilla extract
- 1 cup boiling water
- 1 cup heavy cream
- 8 oz semi-sweet chocolate chips
- 2 tbsp unsalted butter
- 1 tsp instant coffee (optional)
- Fresh berries (for garnish, optional)

Substitutions

- You can use dark chocolate for a richer flavor.
- Add a teaspoon of cinnamon for a hint of spice.

Directions

1. Preheat your oven to 350°F (175°C) and grease two 9-inch round cake pans.
2. In a large mixing bowl, sift together flour, sugar, cocoa powder, baking powder, baking soda, and salt.
3. Add eggs, milk, vegetable oil, and vanilla extract to the dry ingredients and mix until well combined.
4. Stir in the boiling water until the batter is smooth (the batter will be thin).
5. Pour the batter evenly into the prepared cake pans.
6. Bake for 30-35 minutes or until a toothpick inserted into the center comes out clean.
7. Let the cakes cool in the pans for 10 minutes, then remove them from the pans and let them cool completely on a wire rack.
8. In a saucepan, heat the heavy cream until it simmers. Remove from heat.
9. Add chocolate chips, butter, and instant coffee (if using) to the hot cream. Let it sit for a minute, then whisk until smooth and glossy.
10. Allow the ganache to cool slightly.
11. Place one cake layer on a serving platter and pour a portion of the ganache over it. Spread it evenly.
12. Place the second cake layer on top and pour the remaining ganache over the entire cake, letting it drip down the sides.
13. If desired, garnish with fresh berries.
14. Slice and enjoy the heavenly Peruvian Chocolate Cake!

24 alfajores

180 cal

60 mins

Peruvian Alfajores

Peruvian Alfajores are delicate sandwich cookies filled with dulce de leche and dusted with powdered sugar.

Ingredients:

- 1 1/2 cups all-purpose flour
- 1/2 cup cornstarch
- 1/2 cup powdered sugar
- 1/4 tsp salt
- 1 cup unsalted butter, softened
- 1 tsp vanilla extract
- Dulce de leche (for filling)
- Powdered sugar (for dusting)

Directions

1. In a bowl, sift together flour, cornstarch, powdered sugar, and salt.
2. In another bowl, cream together softened butter and vanilla extract until smooth and fluffy.
3. Gradually add the dry ingredients to the butter mixture and mix until a soft dough forms.
4. Shape the dough into a ball, wrap it in plastic wrap, and refrigerate for 30 minutes.
5. Preheat your oven to 350°F (175°C).
6. Roll out the chilled dough on a floured surface to about 1/4-inch thickness.
7. Use a cookie cutter to cut out rounds or desired shapes.
8. Place the cookies on a baking sheet lined with parchment paper.
9. Bake for 10-12 minutes or until the edges are lightly golden.
10. Let the cookies cool completely.
11. Spread dulce de leche on the bottom side of one cookie and sandwich it with another cookie.
12. Dust the alfajores with powdered sugar.
13. Enjoy these delightful Peruvian Alfajores with a cup of coffee or tea!

Substitutions

- You can add shredded coconut to the dulce de leche for extra flavor.

6 servings

220 cal

60 mins

Easy

Peruvian Mazamorra Morada

Mazamorra Morada is a sweet Peruvian dessert made from purple corn and flavored with spices and dried fruits.

Ingredients:

- 1 cup purple corn kernels
- 4 cups water
- 2 cinnamon sticks
- 4 cloves
- 1/2 cup dried pineapple chunks
- 1/2 cup dried apricots
- 1/2 cup dried prunes
- 1/2 cup sweet potato chunks
- 1/2 cup canned purple corn kernels (optional, for texture)
- 1 cup sugar
- 1/4 cup cornstarch
- 1 tsp vanilla extract
- Ground cinnamon (for garnish, optional)

Substitutions

- You can add raisins or other dried fruits of your choice.
- Adjust the sugar to your preferred level of sweetness.

Directions

1. In a large pot, combine purple corn kernels and water. Bring to a boil, then reduce heat and simmer for about 30 minutes, or until the liquid becomes purple and fragrant.
2. Strain the liquid to remove the corn kernels, returning the liquid to the pot.
3. Add cinnamon sticks, cloves, dried pineapple chunks, dried apricots, dried prunes, and sweet potato chunks to the pot. Simmer for an additional 20 minutes or until the fruits and sweet potatoes are tender.
4. In a separate bowl, mix cornstarch with a small amount of cold water to make a slurry.
5. Slowly pour the cornstarch slurry into the pot, stirring constantly to thicken the mixture.
6. Add sugar and continue to cook, stirring, until the Mazamorra Morada thickens to your desired consistency.
7. Remove the pot from heat and stir in vanilla extract.
8. Let the dessert cool to room temperature.
9. Serve in bowls, garnished with ground cinnamon if desired.
10. Enjoy the sweet and spiced Peruvian Mazamorra Morada!

8 servings

280 cal

90 mins

Peruvian Flan

Peruvian Flan is a creamy caramel custard dessert with a smooth texture and rich caramel sauce.

Ingredients:

- 1 cup granulated sugar
- 6 large eggs
- 1 can (14 oz) sweetened condensed milk
- 1 can (12 oz) evaporated milk
- 1 tsp vanilla extract
- 1/4 tsp salt

Directions

1. Preheat your oven to 350°F (175°C).
2. In a saucepan, melt granulated sugar over medium heat, stirring constantly until it turns into a golden caramel. Be careful not to burn it.
3. Quickly pour the caramel into the bottom of a round or rectangular baking dish, swirling it to coat the bottom evenly. Let it cool and harden.
4. In a blender, combine eggs, sweetened condensed milk, evaporated milk, vanilla extract, and salt. Blend until smooth.
5. Carefully pour the milk mixture over the caramel layer in the baking dish.
6. Place the baking dish in a larger roasting pan and fill the roasting pan with hot water until it reaches halfway up the sides of the baking dish (this is called a water bath or bain-marie).
7. Cover the baking dish loosely with aluminum foil.
8. Bake in the preheated oven for 50-60 minutes or until the flan is set but still slightly jiggly in the center.
9. Remove the baking dish from the water bath and let it cool to room temperature.
10. Once cooled, refrigerate the flan for at least 4 hours or overnight.
11. To serve, run a knife around the edge of the baking dish to loosen the flan.
12. Place a serving platter upside down over the dish and carefully flip it over to release the flan with the caramel sauce on top.
13. Slice and enjoy the velvety Peruvian Flan!

Substitutions

- You can add a touch of cinnamon or lemon zest to the custard for extra flavor.
- Experiment with different shapes and sizes of molds for presentation.

6 servings

220 cal

60 mins

Easy

Peruvian Rice Pudding (Arroz con Leche)

Arroz con Leche is a comforting Peruvian rice pudding flavored with cinnamon and sweetened with condensed milk.

Ingredients:

- 1 cup white rice
- 4 cups water
- 1 cinnamon stick
- 4 cups whole milk
- 1 can (14 oz) sweetened condensed milk
- 1 tsp vanilla extract
- Ground cinnamon (for garnish, optional)

Directions

1. In a saucepan, combine white rice, water, and the cinnamon stick. Bring to a boil, then reduce heat and simmer for about 20-25 minutes, or until the rice is tender and the water is absorbed.
2. Add whole milk, sweetened condensed milk, and vanilla extract to the rice. Stir well.
3. Simmer the mixture over low heat, stirring frequently, for another 20-25 minutes, or until the rice pudding thickens and reaches your desired consistency.
4. Remove the cinnamon stick.
5. Remove the pot from heat and let the rice pudding cool slightly.
6. Serve in bowls, garnished with a sprinkle of ground cinnamon if desired.
7. Enjoy the warm and comforting Peruvian Arroz con Leche!

Substitutions

- You can add raisins or lemon zest for extra flavor.
- Adjust the sweetness by adding more or less sweetened condensed milk.

6 servings

320 cal

60 mins

Peruvian Suspiro a la Limeña

Suspiro a la Limeña is a sweet Peruvian dessert consisting of creamy caramel and a velvety meringue topping.

Ingredients:

- 1 can (14 oz) sweetened condensed milk
- 4 large egg yolks
- 1 tsp vanilla extract
- 1/2 cup white wine (Pisco or port wine)
- 1 cup granulated sugar
- 1/4 cup water
- 4 large egg whites
- Ground cinnamon (for garnish, optional)
- Cinnamon sticks (for garnish, optional)

Substitutions

- You can use brandy or rum instead of white wine for a different flavor.
- Torch the meringue topping for a toasted finish.

Directions

1. In a saucepan, combine sweetened condensed milk, egg yolks, and vanilla extract. Cook over low heat, stirring constantly, until the mixture thickens and comes away from the sides of the pan. This will take about 20-30 minutes. Remove from heat and let it cool.
2. In another saucepan, heat white wine over low heat until it reduces by half. Remove from heat and let it cool.
3. In a separate saucepan, combine granulated sugar and water. Cook over low heat, swirling the pan occasionally, until it turns into a golden caramel. Be careful not to burn it.
4. Carefully pour the caramel into the bottom of dessert glasses or bowls, swirling to coat the bottom evenly. Let it cool and harden.
5. Once the caramel is set, spoon a layer of the sweetened condensed milk mixture on top.
6. In a bowl, beat egg whites until stiff peaks form.
7. Gradually fold the reduced white wine into the beaten egg whites.
8. Spoon the meringue over the sweetened condensed milk layer.
9. If desired, garnish with ground cinnamon and cinnamon sticks.
10. Refrigerate the desserts for at least 1 hour before serving.
11. Enjoy the delightful and airy Peruvian Suspiro a la Limeña!

12 servings

280 cal

90 mins

Peruvian Turron de Doña Pepa

Turron de Doña Pepa is a traditional Peruvian dessert made of layers of anise-flavored cookies and sweet honey syrup.

Ingredients:

- 3 cups all-purpose flour
- 1/2 tsp baking soda
- 1 tsp anise seeds
- 1/2 tsp salt
- 1/2 cup unsalted butter, softened
- 1/2 cup granulated sugar
- 1/4 cup evaporated milk
- 1/4 cup anise liqueur (such as anisette)
- 1/2 tsp anise extract
- Vegetable oil (for frying)
- 1/2 cup honey
- 1/4 cup granulated sugar
- 1/4 cup water
- Sprinkles (for decoration, optional)

Substitutions

- You can use anise extract if anise liqueur is not available.
- Customize the sprinkles to match the colors of your celebration.

Directions

1. In a bowl, whisk together flour, baking soda, anise seeds, and salt.
2. In a separate large mixing bowl, cream together softened butter and granulated sugar until light and fluffy.
3. Add evaporated milk, anise liqueur, and anise extract to the butter mixture. Mix until well combined.
4. Gradually add the dry ingredients to the wet ingredients and mix until a soft dough forms.
5. Cover the dough and let it rest for 30 minutes.
6. Preheat vegetable oil in a deep frying pan or skillet.
7. Roll out the dough on a floured surface to about 1/4-inch thickness.
8. Use a knife or cookie cutter to cut out strips or desired shapes.
9. Fry the strips in batches until golden brown and crispy, about 2-3 minutes per side.
10. Drain the fried strips on paper towels.
11. In a saucepan, combine honey, granulated sugar, and water. Cook over low heat, stirring constantly, until the mixture thickens into a syrup (about 15 minutes).
12. Dip the fried strips into the honey syrup, making sure they are well coated.
13. Place the syrup-coated strips on a wire rack to let the excess syrup drip off.
14. If desired, decorate with sprinkles while the syrup is still tacky.
15. Let the Turron de Doña Pepa cool and harden before serving.
16. Enjoy this festive and sweet Peruvian dessert!

6 servings

250 cal

60 mins

Peruvian Chocolate Mousse (Mazamorra de Chocolate)

Easy

Mazamorra de Chocolate is a delightful Peruvian chocolate mousse made with rich dark chocolate and a touch of cinnamon.

Ingredients:

- 7 oz dark chocolate (70% cocoa), chopped
- 1/4 cup unsweetened cocoa powder
- 1/2 cup granulated sugar
- 2 cups whole milk
- 1/4 cup cornstarch
- 1/2 tsp ground cinnamon
- 1 tsp vanilla extract
- Whipped cream (for garnish, optional)
- Chocolate shavings (for garnish, optional)

Directions

1. In a bowl, mix together cocoa powder, granulated sugar, cornstarch, and ground cinnamon. Set aside.
2. In a saucepan, heat 1 cup of whole milk over medium heat until it simmers.
3. Gradually whisk the dry ingredients mixture into the hot milk until it thickens and becomes smooth.
4. Remove the saucepan from heat and stir in the chopped dark chocolate until fully melted.
5. Add the remaining cup of whole milk and vanilla extract, stirring until well combined.
6. Transfer the mixture to a blender and blend until smooth.
7. Pour the chocolate mousse into individual serving glasses or bowls.
8. Refrigerate for at least 4 hours or until set.
9. Garnish with a dollop of whipped cream and chocolate shavings if desired.
10. Enjoy the velvety Peruvian Chocolate Mousse!

Substitutions

- You can add a splash of Pisco (Peruvian brandy) for an adult version.
- Top with fresh berries for a fruity twist.

Chapter 10:
Desserts - Fruits and Nuts

4 servings

150 cal

20 mins

Easy

Peruvian Fruit Salad (Ensalada de Frutas)

Peruvian Fruit Salad is a refreshing blend of tropical fruits with a zesty lime and honey dressing.

Ingredients:

- 1 cup diced pineapple
- 1 cup diced mango
- 1 cup diced papaya
- 1 cup diced watermelon
- 1/4 cup fresh lime juice
- 2 tbsp honey
- Fresh mint leaves (for garnish, optional)

Directions

1. In a large bowl, combine diced pineapple, mango, papaya, and watermelon.
2. In a separate small bowl, whisk together fresh lime juice and honey until well combined.
3. Drizzle the lime and honey dressing over the fruit.
4. Gently toss to coat the fruit in the dressing.
5. Garnish with fresh mint leaves if desired.
6. Serve the Peruvian Fruit Salad immediately and enjoy the burst of tropical flavors!

Substitutions

- You can add diced bananas or strawberries for more variety.
- Adjust the sweetness and tanginess of the dressing to your taste.

12 picarones | 230 cal | 90 mins

Peruvian Picarones

Picarones are sweet potato and pumpkin doughnuts served with a spiced syrup made from chancaca.

Ingredients:

- 1 cup sweet potato, cooked and mashed
- 1 cup pumpkin puree
- 2 cups all-purpose flour
- 1 packet (7g) active dry yeast
- 1/4 cup lukewarm water
- 1/2 tsp salt
- 1/4 tsp anise seeds
- Vegetable oil (for frying)
- Chancaca (unrefined cane sugar) or dark brown sugar (for the syrup)
- Ground cinnamon (for garnish, optional)

Directions

1. In a small bowl, dissolve active dry yeast in lukewarm water and let it sit for about 5 minutes until foamy.
2. In a large mixing bowl, combine mashed sweet potato and pumpkin puree.
3. Add the activated yeast mixture to the sweet potato and pumpkin, and mix well.
4. Gradually add all-purpose flour, salt, and anise seeds to the mixture, kneading until you have a smooth dough.
5. Cover the dough and let it rise in a warm place for about 1 hour or until it has doubled in size.
6. In a deep frying pan or skillet, heat vegetable oil over medium heat.
7. Wet your hands and shape the dough into rings or figure-eight shapes.
8. Carefully drop the picarones into the hot oil and fry until they are golden brown and cooked through, about 4-5 minutes per side.
9. Remove the picarones from the oil and drain them on paper towels.
10. In a saucepan, melt chancaca or dark brown sugar over low heat until it becomes a syrup.
11. Dip the picarones into the warm syrup, coating them evenly.
12. If desired, sprinkle ground cinnamon over the picarones.
13. Serve the sweet and syrupy Peruvian Picarones while they are still warm!

Substitutions

- You can use butternut squash instead of pumpkin for a slightly different flavor.
- If chancaca is not available, use dark brown sugar or molasses for the syrup.

4 servings

160 cal

20 mins

Peruvian Fried Plantains (Plátanos Fritos)

Peruvian Fried Plantains are a beloved snack or side dish, showcasing the natural sweetness of ripe plantains.

Ingredients:

- 2 ripe plantains, peeled and sliced into diagonal pieces
- Vegetable oil (for frying)
- Salt (optional)

Directions

1. In a deep frying pan or skillet, heat vegetable oil over medium-high heat.
2. Carefully add the sliced plantains to the hot oil.
3. Fry the plantains until they are golden brown and caramelized, about 2-3 minutes per side.
4. Remove the plantains from the oil and drain them on paper towels.
5. If desired, sprinkle a pinch of salt over the hot fried plantains.
6. Serve the Peruvian Fried Plantains as a delightful snack or side dish!

Substitutions

- You can dust the fried plantains with powdered sugar for a sweet twist.
- Serve with a drizzle of honey or a sprinkle of cinnamon for added flavor.

4 caramel apples

280 cal

30 mins

Peruvian Caramel Apples (Manzanas con Leche)

Peruvian Caramel Apples are a delightful treat featuring crisp apples coated in creamy caramel and chocolate.

Ingredients:

- 4 apples (Granny Smith or your favorite variety)
- 1 cup granulated sugar
- 1/4 cup water
- 1/2 cup heavy cream
- 1/4 cup unsalted butter
- 1/4 cup chocolate chips (optional)
- Chopped nuts or sprinkles (for decoration, optional)

Directions

1. Wash and thoroughly dry the apples. Remove the stems and insert wooden sticks into the tops.
2. In a saucepan, combine granulated sugar and water. Cook over medium-high heat, swirling the pan occasionally, until it turns into a golden caramel.
3. Carefully dip each apple into the hot caramel, swirling to coat them evenly. Let any excess caramel drip off.
4. Place the caramel-coated apples on a parchment-lined baking sheet to cool and harden.
5. In another saucepan, heat heavy cream and unsalted butter over low heat until the butter is melted and the mixture is hot but not boiling.
6. Add chocolate chips to the cream mixture and stir until the chocolate is fully melted and smooth (if using).
7. Drizzle the caramel-coated apples with the chocolate sauce.
8. If desired, decorate the caramel apples with chopped nuts or colorful sprinkles while the chocolate is still tacky.
9. Let the caramel and chocolate set before enjoying your Peruvian Caramel Apples!

Substitutions

- You can roll the caramel-coated apples in crushed cookies, nuts, or shredded coconut for added texture.
- Experiment with different types of chocolate for the drizzle.

About 2 cups

40 cal

45 mins

Peruvian Guava Jelly (Dulce de Guayaba)

Peruvian Guava Jelly is a sweet spread made from guava fruit, often enjoyed with bread or crackers.

Ingredients:

- 8 ripe guava fruits
- 2 cups granulated sugar
- 1/2 cup water
- 1 tsp lemon juice

Directions

1. Wash the guava fruits and cut off the ends. Quarter the guavas.
2. In a large pot, combine guava quarters, granulated sugar, water, and lemon juice.
3. Bring the mixture to a boil over medium-high heat, then reduce the heat and simmer for about 30-35 minutes, or until the guava fruit is soft and can be easily mashed with a fork.
4. Remove the pot from heat and let it cool slightly.
5. Use a potato masher or a food processor to blend the guava mixture until smooth.
6. Return the pot to low heat and simmer for an additional 10-15 minutes, stirring constantly, until the guava jelly thickens.
7. Remove from heat and let the guava jelly cool to room temperature.
8. Transfer the guava jelly to clean, sterilized jars with airtight lids.
9. Store the Peruvian Guava Jelly in the refrigerator and use it as a delicious spread!

Substitutions

- You can strain the guava mixture to remove seeds if you prefer a seedless jelly.
- Adjust the sugar to your preferred level of sweetness.

2 servings

120 cal

10 mins

Easy

Peruvian Fruit Smoothie (Jugo de Frutas)

Jugo de Frutas is a simple and refreshing Peruvian fruit smoothie made with a blend of tropical fruits.

Ingredients:

- 1/2 cup diced papaya
- 1/2 cup diced mango
- 1/2 cup diced pineapple
- 1/2 cup diced orange
- 1/2 cup diced banana
- 1/2 cup water
- 2 tbsp honey (optional)
- Ice cubes (optional)

Directions

1. In a blender, combine diced papaya, mango, pineapple, orange, and banana.
2. Add water and honey (if using) to the blender.
3. Blend until the mixture is smooth and all the ingredients are well combined.
4. If desired, add ice cubes to the blender and blend until the smoothie is chilled and slightly frothy.
5. Pour the Peruvian Fruit Smoothie into glasses and serve immediately for a refreshing taste of Peru!

Substitutions

- Customize your smoothie by adding yogurt or milk for a creamier texture.
- Adjust the sweetness with honey or sugar according to your taste.

About 2 cups

80 cal

90 mins

Peruvian Quince Paste (Dulce de Membrillo)

Dulce de Membrillo is a sweet and firm quince paste that is often enjoyed with cheese or crackers.

Ingredients:

- 4 large quince fruits
- 2 cups granulated sugar
- 1/2 cup water
- 1/2 tsp lemon juice

Directions

1. Wash and peel the quince fruits. Remove the cores and cut them into chunks.
2. In a large pot, combine quince chunks, granulated sugar, water, and lemon juice.
3. Bring the mixture to a boil over medium-high heat, then reduce the heat and simmer for about 60-75 minutes, or until the quince is soft and the liquid has reduced significantly.
4. Remove the pot from heat and let it cool slightly.
5. Use a food processor or blender to puree the quince mixture until smooth.
6. Return the puree to the pot and cook over low heat, stirring constantly, for an additional 10-15 minutes until it thickens and pulls away from the sides of the pot.
7. Remove from heat and let the quince paste cool to room temperature.
8. Cut the quince paste into squares or desired shapes.
9. Store the Peruvian Quince Paste in an airtight container at room temperature or in the refrigerator.
10. Enjoy it with cheese or crackers!

Substitutions

- You can add a touch of cinnamon or vanilla extract for extra flavor.
- Store the quince paste in the refrigerator for longer shelf life.

About 2 cups | 160 cal | 40 mins

Easy

Peruvian Candied Nuts (Maní Confite)

Maní Confite are sweet and crunchy candied peanuts, a popular street snack in Peru.

Ingredients:

- 2 cups raw peanuts
- 1 cup granulated sugar
- 1/4 cup water
- 1/2 tsp vanilla extract
- 1/4 tsp salt
- 1/4 tsp ground cinnamon (optional)
- 1/4 tsp ground cloves (optional)

Directions

1. In a large non-stick skillet, combine raw peanuts, granulated sugar, water, vanilla extract, salt, and ground cinnamon and cloves (if using).
2. Cook over medium heat, stirring constantly, until the sugar melts and coats the peanuts evenly. This will take about 10-15 minutes.
3. Continue to cook and stir until the sugar crystallizes and turns into a white powder coating the peanuts. This will take another 10-15 minutes.
4. Remove the skillet from heat and let the candied peanuts cool slightly.
5. Separate the peanuts by breaking them apart with a spatula or your fingers.
6. Once completely cooled, store the Peruvian Candied Nuts in an airtight container at room temperature.
7. Enjoy this sweet and crunchy street snack!

Substitutions

- Add a pinch of cayenne pepper for a spicy kick.
- Experiment with different nuts like almonds or cashews.

12 strawberries | 150 cal | 30 mins

Peruvian Chocolate-Covered Strawberries

Peruvian Chocolate-Covered Strawberries are a romantic and indulgent treat for any special occasion.

Ingredients:

- 12 fresh strawberries
- 4 oz dark chocolate, chopped
- 2 oz white chocolate, chopped (optional)
- Sprinkles or chopped nuts (for decoration, optional)

Directions

1. Wash and thoroughly dry the strawberries, leaving the stems on.
2. In separate microwave-safe bowls, melt the dark chocolate and white chocolate (if using) in 20-second intervals, stirring each time until smooth.
3. Hold each strawberry by the stem and dip it into the melted dark chocolate, swirling to coat it evenly.
4. Place the chocolate-covered strawberry on a parchment-lined tray.
5. If using white chocolate, drizzle it over the dark chocolate-coated strawberries for a decorative touch.
6. If desired, decorate with colorful sprinkles or chopped nuts while the chocolate is still tacky.
7. Allow the chocolate to set before serving.
8. Share these delightful Peruvian Chocolate-Covered Strawberries with your loved ones!

Substitutions

- Experiment with different types of chocolate for a variety of flavors.
- Drizzle caramel sauce over the strawberries for an extra layer of sweetness.

24 cookies

100 cal

45 mins

Peruvian Walnut Cookies (Pan de Pasas)

Pan de Pasas are delightful Peruvian walnut cookies studded with raisins and flavored with spices.

Ingredients:

- 1 cup all-purpose flour
- 1/2 cup unsalted butter, softened
- 1/2 cup granulated sugar
- 1 egg
- 1/2 cup chopped walnuts
- 1/2 cup raisins
- 1/2 tsp ground cinnamon
- 1/4 tsp ground cloves
- 1/4 tsp salt
- 1/4 tsp baking powder
- 1/4 tsp baking soda

Directions

1. Preheat your oven to 350°F (175°C) and line a baking sheet with parchment paper.
2. In a bowl, whisk together all-purpose flour, ground cinnamon, ground cloves, salt, baking powder, and baking soda.
3. In another mixing bowl, cream together softened unsalted butter and granulated sugar until light and fluffy.
4. Add an egg to the butter-sugar mixture and beat until well combined.
5. Gradually add the dry ingredients to the wet ingredients and mix until a cookie dough forms.
6. Stir in chopped walnuts and raisins until evenly distributed throughout the dough.
7. Drop spoonfuls of cookie dough onto the prepared baking sheet, spacing them apart.
8. Bake for about 12-15 minutes, or until the cookies are golden brown at the edges.
9. Remove the cookies from the oven and let them cool on the baking sheet for a few minutes before transferring them to a wire rack to cool completely.
10. Enjoy the warm and nutty Peruvian Walnut Cookies!

Substitutions

- Customize the cookie dough by adding chocolate chips or dried cranberries.
- Use pecans or almonds instead of walnuts for a different nutty flavor.

Chapter 11:
Beverages

4 servings | 80 cal | 60 mins

Peruvian Chicha Morada

Chicha Morada is a vibrant and refreshing Peruvian drink made from purple corn, pineapple, and spices.

Ingredients:

- 2 cups purple corn kernels (dried)
- 8 cups water
- 1 pineapple, peeled and chopped
- 1 cinnamon stick
- 4 cloves
- 1/4 cup fresh lime juice
- Sugar or honey (to taste)
- Ice cubes (optional)

Directions

1. In a large pot, combine purple corn kernels and water.
2. Bring to a boil over medium-high heat, then reduce the heat and simmer for about 45 minutes, or until the liquid turns a deep purple color.
3. Remove from heat and strain the liquid into a pitcher, discarding the corn kernels.
4. In the same pot, combine the strained purple corn liquid, chopped pineapple, cinnamon stick, and cloves.
5. Simmer for an additional 15 minutes to infuse the flavors.
6. Remove from heat and let it cool to room temperature.
7. Stir in fresh lime juice and sweeten with sugar or honey to taste.
8. Chill in the refrigerator.
9. Serve the Peruvian Chicha Morada over ice cubes for a refreshing drink!

Substitutions

- Adjust the sweetness to your preference with sugar or honey.
- Add a few slices of fresh pineapple to the pitcher for extra flavor.
- Garnish with a sprig of fresh mint if desired.

2 servings

220 cal

10 mins

Peruvian Pisco Sour

Pisco Sour is Peru's national cocktail, a delightful blend of pisco brandy, lime juice, simple syrup, and egg white foam.

Ingredients:

- 3 oz pisco brandy
- 1 oz fresh lime juice
- 1 oz simple syrup
- 1/2 oz pasteurized egg white
- Angostura bitters (for garnish, optional)
- Ice cubes

Directions

1. Fill a cocktail shaker with ice cubes.
2. Add pisco brandy, fresh lime juice, simple syrup, and pasteurized egg white to the shaker.
3. Shake vigorously for about 15-20 seconds until well-chilled and frothy.
4. Strain the cocktail into chilled glasses.
5. If desired, add a few drops of Angostura bitters on top for a decorative touch.
6. Serve the classic Peruvian Pisco Sour immediately and savor its unique flavor!

Substitutions

- You can use freshly squeezed lemon juice for a slightly different citrus flavor.
- Adjust the sweetness of the simple syrup to your taste.

2 servings

220 cal

5 mins

Easy

Peruvian Inca Kola

Inca Kola is a popular Peruvian soft drink with a unique and vibrant flavor that combines lemon verbena and bubblegum.

Ingredients:

- 12 oz Inca Kola (or any cream soda if unavailable)
- Ice cubes
- Lemon slices (for garnish, optional)

Directions

1. Fill a glass with ice cubes.
2. Pour chilled Inca Kola over the ice.
3. Garnish with a lemon slice if desired.
4. Enjoy the fizzy and distinctive Peruvian Inca Kola!

Substitutions

- If Inca Kola is not available, you can use cream soda with a touch of lemon juice for a similar taste.
- Adjust the sweetness and lemon flavor to your preference.

2 servings

5 cal

10 mins

Peruvian Coffee (Café Peruano)

Café Peruano is a simple and aromatic Peruvian coffee made from high-quality coffee beans, water, and love.

Ingredients:

- 2 cups hot water
- 4 tbsp ground Peruvian coffee beans (medium roast)
- Sugar or sweeteners (to taste)
- Cream or milk (optional)

Directions

1. Place ground Peruvian coffee beans in a coffee filter within a drip coffee maker or a French press.
2. Heat water until it's just below boiling, around 200°F (93°C).
3. Slowly pour hot water over the coffee grounds, allowing it to steep for about 4-5 minutes.
4. Remove the coffee filter or press the plunger down in the French press to separate the grounds from the liquid.
5. Pour the Peruvian Coffee into cups.
6. Sweeten with sugar or sweeteners to taste, and add cream or milk if desired.
7. Savor the rich aroma and flavor of Café Peruano!

Substitutions

- Choose coffee beans of your preferred roast level for different flavor profiles.
- Customize with flavored syrups like vanilla or caramel for a unique twist.

2 servings

5 cal

10 mins

Peruvian Herbal Tea (Mate de Hierbas)

Mate de Hierbas is a soothing Peruvian herbal tea made from a blend of fragrant herbs like chamomile and lemon verbena.

Ingredients:

- 2 cups hot water
- 2 tbsp dried chamomile flowers
- 2 tbsp dried lemon verbena leaves
- Honey or lemon slices (for flavor, optional)

Directions

1. In a teapot or heatproof container, combine dried chamomile flowers and dried lemon verbena leaves.
2. Pour hot water over the herbs.
3. Let the tea steep for about 5-7 minutes, or until it reaches your preferred strength.
4. Strain the tea into cups.
5. Sweeten with honey or add lemon slices for extra flavor if desired.
6. Enjoy the calming and aromatic Peruvian Herbal Tea!

Substitutions

- Experiment with other herbs like mint or lemongrass for different herbal flavors.
- Adjust the sweetness and citrus notes to your liking.

4 servings

160 cal

30 mins

Peruvian Quince Punch (Jugo de Membrillo)

Jugo de Membrillo is a sweet and tangy Peruvian quince punch that combines quince fruit, sugar, and a hint of cinnamon.

Ingredients:

- 2 large quince fruits, peeled and diced
- 4 cups water
- 1 cup granulated sugar
- 1 cinnamon stick
- Lime juice (to taste)
- Ice cubes (optional)

Directions

1. In a large pot, combine diced quince fruits and water.
2. Add granulated sugar and a cinnamon stick to the pot.
3. Bring the mixture to a boil over medium-high heat, then reduce the heat and simmer for about 20-25 minutes, or until the quince is soft and the liquid thickens slightly.
4. Remove from heat and let it cool to room temperature.
5. Remove the cinnamon stick and blend the quince mixture until smooth.
6. Strain the quince puree into a pitcher.
7. Add lime juice to taste, adjusting the sweetness if needed.
8. Chill the Peruvian Quince Punch in the refrigerator.
9. Serve over ice cubes for a refreshing quince beverage!

Substitutions

- You can vary the level of sweetness with more or less sugar.
- Experiment with other spices like cloves for a different flavor twist.

2 servings

140 cal

10 mins

Peruvian Passion Fruit Juice (Jugo de Maracuyá)

Easy

Jugo de Maracuyá is a tropical Peruvian passion fruit juice bursting with tangy and sweet flavors.

Ingredients:

- 4 ripe passion fruits
- 1/4 cup granulated sugar
- 1/2 cup water
- Ice cubes (optional)

Directions

1. Cut the passion fruits in half and scoop out the pulp and seeds into a blender.
2. Add granulated sugar and water to the blender.
3. Blend on high speed until the mixture is smooth.
4. Strain the passion fruit juice through a fine mesh strainer to remove seeds.
5. Chill in the refrigerator or serve immediately over ice cubes.
6. Enjoy the delightful Peruvian Passion Fruit Juice!

Substitutions

- Adjust the sweetness to your taste by adding more or less sugar.
- If you enjoy the crunch of passion fruit seeds, skip the straining step.

A small favor to ask

Dear aficionados of Peruvian cuisine and fellow culinary explorers,

As we savor the final bites of our gastronomic journey within the pages of the "Peruvian Comforts Cookbook: Savor Peruvian Flavors - 100+ Authentic Recipes," I want to extend my heartfelt gratitude for joining me on this flavorful adventure. Together, we've embarked on a culinary expedition into the heart and soul of Peru's rich culinary heritage, bringing the delectable flavors of Peru to your very own kitchen.

Now, I come to you with a humble request, one that carries profound significance for us —a small but passionate publishing team. Reviews, in the world of cookbooks, are like the secret ingredients that elevate a dish from good to extraordinary. They are as elusive as the melodies of Andean panpipes, yet they are the lifeblood of our creative spirit.

If these recipes have allowed you to savor the authentic and vibrant tastes of Peru while simplifying the process with readily available ingredients, I would be eternally grateful if you could spare a moment. Please return to the app or platform where you acquired this book, and there, you'll find a review button waiting for your input. A star rating and a brief sentence sharing your thoughts would be the culinary equivalent of a standing ovation in our world.

You see, as a small publisher, every review is a guiding star that illuminates our path. Your words have the power to inspire others to embark on their own Peruvian culinary journey, recreating the rich and flavorful dishes of Peru within the comfort of their own homes.

Rest assured, every review is not just welcomed but treasured. We understand that, even in the most skilled kitchens, the most talented chefs may occasionally make a minor mistake. If you happen to spot any such hiccup along the way, please understand that we've poured our hearts into this cookbook. We're human, and in the world of cooking, a touch of imperfection is part of the magic.

From the depths of my heart, thank you for choosing the "Peruvian Comforts Cookbook," and thank you in advance for considering leaving a review. Your support fuels our passion for creating more delectable, authentic, and accessible culinary experiences. Until we meet again in the pages of another cookbook, may your culinary adventures continue to be filled with the vibrant and soulful flavors of Peru, the joy of home cooking, and the shared delight of meals with loved ones. ¡Buen provecho! (Bon appétit!)